Essential Staff Training Activities

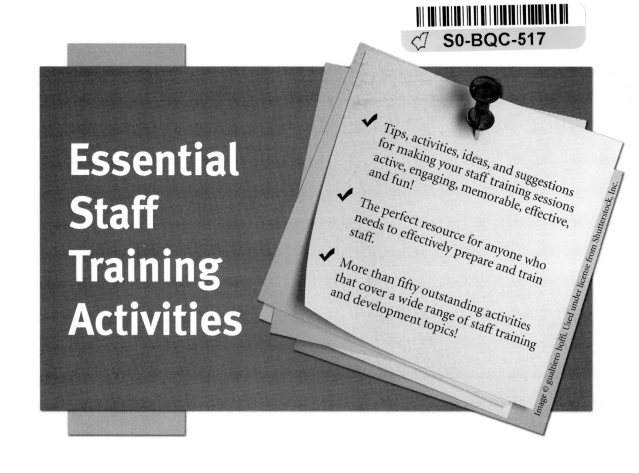

✔ Tips, activities, ideas, and suggestions for making your staff training sessions active, engaging, memorable, effective, and fun!

✔ The perfect resource for anyone who needs to effectively prepare and train staff.

✔ More than fifty outstanding activities that cover a wide range of staff training and development topics!

Image © gualtiero boffi. Used under license from Shutterstock, Inc.

Jim Cain
Clare-Marie Hannon
Dave Knobbe
With Foreword by Michael Brandwein

A Teamwork & Teamplay Publication

Building Unity, Community, Connection, Leadership, Engagement & Teamwork Through Active Learning

KENDALL/HUNT PUBLISHING COMPANY
4050 Westmark Drive   Dubuque, Iowa 52002

SEND PERMISSION INQUIRIES TO:

Jim Cain
Teamwork & Teamplay
c/o Kendall/Hunt Publishing Company
Permissions Department
4050 Westmark Drive
Dubuque, IA 52002
563-589-7017
Email: permissions@kendallhunt.com

SEND INQUIRIES ABOUT OUR PUBLICATIONS TO:

Jim Cain
Teamwork & Teamplay
468 Salmon Creek Road
Brockport, NY 14420
(585) 637-0328
Email: jimcain@teamworkandteamplay.com
Website: www.teamworkandteamplay.com

Cover image © Luminis, 2008
Image used under license from Shutterstock, Inc.

Printed in the United States of America
10 9 8 7 6 5 4 3 2

Contents

Foreword

My friend and colleague Jim Cain is an exceptionally nice man who also happens to be a masterful trainer with sterling skills. So when he told me he was writing a new book and asked if I would write some brief comments about the importance of using staff training activities to promote active learning, I was happy to do so, even though we both know that I've never been brief in my entire life. In fact, when Jim told me that this new book would be shorter than his earlier *Teamwork & Teamplay*, I secretly thought to myself: "Not if I write the foreword, it won't . . ."

I heard it only when I was in the car.

I was recently driving to a conference. It was late at night, but I was enjoying the music that was playing through the portable music player that I had plugged into the car's sound system. Suddenly, a song shuffled on that I had downloaded recently but had only listened to on my office computer. The two speakers attached to my computer are pretty good, but the stereo separation from the four in my car is apparently even better than I would have guessed. As the song reverberated throughout the car, I was able to hear new instruments and subtleties that I had never noticed when listening in my office.

Staff training activities can be like that song. The first time we experience them, we may not fully appreciate their full value and importance.

When we first see a training activity that incorporates physical movement and play, we may view it as a form of self-defense. "Oh, cool—here's a GAME that I can have staff play in the middle of orientation so I don't have to keep them sitting on these hard benches in 93 degree heat. If I give them this little break—during which they can also learn something—then maybe this afternoon when we have to go over employment policies and procedures, they will be able to suppress the urge to drag me outside and use my body as an element in an obstacle course."

But with a second look at a well-selected, skillfully led training activity, we can discover rich opportunities and benefits that may have escaped earlier notice. There are three key benefits to these activities that make them far more valuable than a fun break. These benefits show how useful these activities can be as part of a well-planned and presented staff development program.

▄▄ Benefit One: It Works

People learn better when they are active, not passive, learners. That's the big payoff from experiential learning: They learn best not when they are lectured, but when they have guided opportunities to discover things themselves. Learning happens when participants can have skillfully led discussions about what happened and how they can apply it to situations in the future.

I wrote in my first book that staff training is most helpfully viewed as teaching, and that identifying the elements of terrific teaching will guide us in providing training that really works. So when we use games and activities that get people out of their seats and actively engaged in their own discovery, we're using one of the very best tools to teach essential staff skills such as communication, collaboration, and problem solving.

▄▄ Benefit Two: It Models for Staff How to Teach and Lead

If we are in the business of training group and team leaders, we want staff to be able to get up in front of a group of people and explain directions clearly and confidently. They need to be able to grab and hold attention and to motivate participation. They have to stimulate and lead useful discussion about the activity to promote learning from what did and did not occur. How do we efficiently and effectively teach these skills to staff?

Watching someone demonstrate an excellent way of doing something is usually better than listening to this person tell us how we should do it ourselves. So when we make active training experiences an integral part of staff development, we provide an opportunity to show and talk about what constitutes great group leadership.

To get this benefit, we have to do two things. First, we have to pay close attention to how we lead the activities for staff. We have to think in advance about the best ways to explain the directions. We must rehearse what we are going to say and how we are going to say it.

Second, we must do more than talk with staff about what they learned as participants in the activity. We must also direct their attention to the techniques that were used to teach it so that they can use these same techniques when leading their own groups. To do this, here are just a few examples of how we can prompt staff to discuss this:

- What are some things that the leader did that made the directions clear?
- What did the leader do and say to hold your attention?
- What things did the leader do or say that were examples of good teaching?

■ Benefit Three: It Provides Opportunities for Many Staff to Develop and Practice Leadership Skills

Have staff training activities led by many different staff, not just senior members of the leadership team. Pair up an experienced activity leader with one or a few staff. Demonstrate or provide a written description of an activity to these persons and ask them to present the activity together during a later staff training session. Be sure that the experienced partner understands the importance of sharing as much responsibility as possible, and that this partner uses preparation time to discuss leadership technique. For example: "If we did it this way, would it be better or weaker teaching than if we did it this way? Why do you think that?"

A big part of squeezing maximum value out of training activities is to have a good start in knowing which ones to lead. Jim Cain and his colleagues Dave Knobbe and Clare-Marie Hannon have combined their expertise and practical know-how to assemble a collection here that will serve as a great resource. Like you, I'm looking forward to studying and learning from them. Let the squeezing begin!

Michael Brandwein
Author of *Training Terrific Staff!*
Volumes 1 & 2

Introduction

During my professional career, I have had the opportunity to work with hundreds of summer camps, youth development agencies, community recreation programs, and a variety of youth and adult leadership programs at colleges, universities, conferences, and workshops around the country and around the world. In almost every situation, the directors operating these facilities and programs engage in a yearly ritual of training new seasonal staff to safely operate and enhance their programs. Many directors say that they can actually predict the success of their program based on the behavior and attitudes of their staff during the initial staff-training program. For some organizations, staff training is a single-day event. For others, it can be a week or more of serious and sometimes strenuous work.

A few years ago, a summer camp staff director asked me to join his camp's staff-training week. He mentioned that working with special populations in a state with many regulations required two full weeks of staff training, and that much of the information communicated during this training event was very dry. My task was to reinforce the necessary components of this training, but to do so in an active and engaging manner. In the end, the director mentioned to me that he would never go back to the way he used to run staff training. Every few hours, we would use one of the activities mentioned in this book to energize and refresh the staff, and to reinforce the key concepts learned during the most recent training session. In the end, this staff retained the necessary information, had more energy and engagement throughout the training program, were united as a team, and were better prepared for the tasks at hand, simply by adding some very valuable active learning opportunities.

As a result of this experience, and many more like it, I have accumulated several dozen activities that I believe are essential to a successful staff-training program. Dave Knobbe and Clare-Marie Hannon, my friends and co-authors on this project, have also contributed their most outstanding ideas, suggestions, references, and activities. Collectively, the three of us have 100 years of experience working with and training seasonal staffs in this country and around the world.

Whether you are training a camp staff, community recreation program staff, youth development staff, resident assistants in university housing, outdoor education leaders, teachers, facilitators, new employees, or indeed, anyone working as part of a team, you need to explore the topics shared in this book and include active learning as part of the required content of your staff-training program. Just remember, though, that the activities themselves are not the end. The discussions that emerge from participating in these activities are where the real teachable moments are found. I hope you enjoy leading and participating in these unique activities with your staff.

Jim Cain

How to Make Your Staff Training Active, Engaging, Memorable, Effective, and Fun!

Let's begin with a simple experiment. Think of a training session or class that you have attended that was absolutely wonderful. Next, think of another session that was very disappointing. No doubt everyone can easily remember a class, training session, or workshop that fits both of these categories. What is most interesting is that it is often not the information being shared that is the contributing factor to whether the class is

good or bad, useful or useless. More often than not, it is the method by which the information is shared that determines whether the participants are engaged in the learning process.

This chapter contains valuable tips, ideas, resources, references, and suggestions for making your staff-training program outstanding. The authors have pulled resources from a variety of educational, training, and learning fields—all with the intent to broaden your perspective on active learning and what your next staff-training program could be. Add to these suggestions some of the activities found in the next three sections, and you'll have a critical mass of tools that are sure to increase the engagement of your staff and help them retain the information you need them to learn.

■ Why Active Learning?

Simply stated, active learning is just that—learning in an active and engaging manner. The role of the teacher becomes that of a facilitator. Knowledge isn't something that is poured into learners, but rather, something they explore and find for themselves. Through the process of inquiry, investigation, group work, discussions, and other active learning opportunities that move beyond lectures and slide presentations, learners are given a more active role in their own education. You expect your staff to think on their feet—so why not train them on the feet? Three experts in education and brain function have this to say about active learning:

As the bottom gets numb-er, the brain gets dumber!
—Marcia L. Tate

Your brain can only absorb what your butt can endure!
—Gabe Campbell

Movement is the door to learning.
—Paul Dennison

By including active learning in your educational and staff-training sessions, you'll engage your participants more deeply by providing a sensory-rich learning environment. Edgar Dale's work on memory and retention of information suggests that the greater the level of involvement or immersion of the student in the learning process, the greater the retention of the information given. Although most forms of conventional learning are somewhat passive (lecture, computer-base learning, PowerPoint presentations, slideshows, reading), there are other choices.

Given the finite amount of time you have to train your staff, and no doubt the extensive amount of material you have to cover during this process, chances are you would

not only like to complete the delivery of the information you have at hand, but ensure that your audience actually retains this information and is able to apply it in the future. Sometimes these two facets (time and the total amount of information) are at odds with each other. You are going to need some help to make this happen, and here it is.

What follows is a collection of tools and techniques that you can use to create a sensory-rich and active learning environment during your staff-training sessions. Remember, the greater the number of methods used to convey information to your staff, the greater their potential for being able to recall this information, and actually applying that knowledge in the right situation, at the right time. Best of all, there are dozens of valuable techniques here, so you can vary the methods you use throughout your staff-training program to keep the information interesting, and the presentation of this information continuously changing and engaging.

The Experiential Learning Process

David Kolb is most often credited with his work related to the experiential learning process, which states that individuals and groups progress through their experiences. One of the greatest educational take-aways from this model is the fact that simply experiencing an educational moment is an incomplete way of learning. Not until the learner has reflected and applied this learning can they be said to have truly *learned* the material presented.

In application to your staff training, it is important not only to share the necessary information and knowledge with your staff, but also to allow them to reflect on this information—and best of all, be given an opportunity to actually use this new knowledge in a genuine situation. Role-plays, practice events, group work, and teach-backs are all helpful ways to prepare your staff to use the knowledge they have gained successfully.

An example of this theory from medical school, is the *see one, do one, teach one* approach to medical procedures. First the students observe. Next they perform the task themselves. Finally, the students achieve the level of ability where they can effectively teach others this skill. The student has truly become the master. Best of all, the students in this scenario are knowledgeable enough to actually use the knowledge they have acquired—just as you would like your staff to do.

Three Primary Forms of Learning (Auditory, Visual, Kinesthetic)

Although additional educational techniques are more common these days, there remain some traditional learning methods that endure because of their value and effectiveness. Auditory techniques include teaching by voice, which includes stories, electronically stored voices, music, books on tape and CD, podcasts, MP3 files, and other person-to-person or electronic means. Sharing your favorite campfire story with your staff is an example of auditory learning. Visual techniques include visual aids such as graphics, illustrations, models, graphs, pictures, and 3-D items that you can pass around the group. The team behavior cards designed by Dave Knobbe in this book are an example of visual models. Kinesthetic learning includes movements of all kinds. Learning how to serve a volleyball and practicing how to tie a knot using a short length of rope are examples of kinesthetic learning.

An example from this book that incorporates all three of these methods is the *Virtual Slideshow* debriefing technique. There is the kinesthetic movement of pointing and clicking the device. There is the auditory clicking sound made by the slideshow clicker. And there is the visual (albeit imaginary) image described by the person operating the clicker. This one technique incorporates all three primary styles of education. How many of your staff-training techniques incorporate more than one primary style of learning?

Multiple Intelligences

Although the work of Howard Gardner is most often credited with defining the current eight accepted styles of multiple intelligences or learning styles, some find this information a bit pedagogical. Thomas Armstrong does an excellent job of interpreting multiple intelligence theory and making it accessible for those of us that would like to utilize these techniques, without obtaining a doctorate degree in education first. The book *Multiple Intelligences in the Classroom,* by Armstrong, is highly recommended.

In this and other sources on multiple-intelligence learning methods, you'll find that there are (currently) eight varieties of intelligences that you can address in your teachings: logical/mathematical, bodily kinesthetic, visual spatial, linguistic, musical, interpersonal (knowledge of others), intrapersonal (knowledge of self), and natural/environmental. In addition, there is some effort underway to include other potential intelligence forms, such as existentialism, mechanical aptitude, and humor.

For many teachers, educators, and trainers, investigating these eight styles, although interesting, is difficult given a standardized curriculum, and impossible given the time provided to explore such techniques. Luckily, active-learning techniques can be used to explore *all* of these intelligences. And best of all, the activities mentioned in this book address all of the multiple intelligence styles (as shown in Table 1.1).

TABLE 1.1

Activities That Work with the Eight Multiple Intelligence Styles

Intelligence/Talent	Active Learning Opportunity	Activities from This Book
Logic/Math	Problem solving skills, analysis, planning	Not Knots, Sunny Side Up
Body-Kinesthetic	Hands-on learning, physical activity, movement	Change Train, Funderbirds
Visual-Spatial	Map reading, visualizing multiple solutions	Not Knots, Bull Ring
Linguistic	Clear expression, reading instructions, debriefing	Quotes in Order, Character Cards
Musical	Rhythm, timing, sounds of nature	Different Drum, Jiffy Mixer
Interpersonal	Understanding, empathy, coaching, teamwork	Trust Drive, 1st Impressions
Intrapersonal	Self analysis, relating, journaling, self-reflection	The Story of Your Name
Nature-Environment	Connection to the outdoor setting, exploring	Anything outside in nature

For more information about multiple intelligence learning, read *Multiple Intelligences in the Classroom,* 2000, Thomas Armstrong, ASCD Alexandria, Virginia USA ISBN 0-87120-376-6) and *Last Child in the Woods—Saving Our Kids from Nature-Deficit Disorder* by Richard Louv (2005, ISBN 978-1565123915) for some additional perspective on the value of outdoor education and the natural world around us. You'll also find additional information on multiple intelligence learning from author Dave Knobbe in Chapter 5 of this book.

■ The Difference Between Short-Term and Long-Term Memory

The difference between short-term and long-term memory is just 20 seconds! That's all, 20 seconds. If you can get your staff to manipulate a concept in their minds for 20 seconds, you can move that concept from their short-term memory to a long-term memory location. Less than 20 seconds— short-term memory. More than 20 seconds—20 years or more.

Consider for yourself—how many times have you been given a telephone number, but before you could write it down, you've lost some of the digits? Chances are, you've forgotten some of those digits before 20 seconds had passed.

One of the activities in this book, *Quotes in Order,* makes use of a group deliberating the correct order of words in a quote they do not yet know. By manipulating the cards containing these words (which generally takes much more than just 20 seconds), the group not only retains the message of the quote, but also can repeat it word for word and will continue to be able to do so now that it resides in their long-term memory.

In regards to your staff-training sessions—any concept that you present for less than 20 seconds is likely to be heard by your staff but unlikely to be retained by them, unless you do something more to engage their memory system. Try the activity *Quotes in Order* found in this book, for your organization's mission statement, vision statement, or goals, and chances are, your staff will remember them long after the activity is completed.

■ Educational Hooks and Triggers

If you have ever forgotten something—the title of a book, a TV character's name, the words to a song, you have probably relied on an educational hook or trigger to help you remember it. That is, remembering one thing helps you remember something else. Educational hooks are just like the hooks that you use to hold the tools in your workshop, your coat in the closet or even your toothbrush in the bathroom. When you

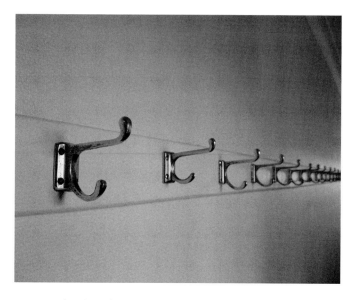

see the appropriate hook, even if the tool, or jacket, or toothbrush is missing, you know what belongs there. There is a connection between the hook and the object that it holds. By remembering the hook, you can also remember what it typically contains.

The Five Finger Rule is a great example of an education hook. The hook is the fingers of your right hand. Each finger represents a simple concept:

- *The thumb—Be positive!* There is enough negativity in the world. You only have to watch the TV or read a newspaper to find it. Let's focus on the good things happening around us. Be positive!
- *The first or pointer finger—Don't point the finger at someone else.* Be responsible for yourself. It is human nature to make mistakes now and then, but we are terrible at covering them up. When you make a mistake, own up to it, and do your best to make it right.
- *The middle finger—It is all about respect.* Everyone deserves it. Everyone!
- *The third or ring finger—Commitment is important.* To the team, to the situation, to the game.
- *The last or pinky finger—Don't forget the little things.* Sometimes, the smallest details can trip us up. Watch out for the little things, and the rest will take care of themselves.

After teaching this simple rule, you can quiz your staff by holding up various fingers and asking them to repeat what each finger represents. They'll most likely be able to tell you each and every concept—because you've given them a very simple hook.

BOX 1.1 The information presented here was shared by a YMCA summer camp staff member from the greater Detroit YMCA. It is not only a valuable thing to teach your staff; it is also an outstanding example of an educational "hook" that can be used to help your staff remember key information.

The concept of an educational trigger is very similar to a hook. One word, phrase, or object helps you remember another important thing. Some bank and computer accounts use this information to assist you in case you forget your password or pin number, by asking such questions as, "What was your mother's maiden name?" Often, before the customer finishes giving the answer to the bank's alternative question, they have remembered the password or pin number. Here are a few educational triggers. Please add the missing word:

Peanut Butter and _____ .
Simon and _____ .
Salt and _____ .
Coffee with cream and _____ .

Here, words and items are used to trigger your memory for another item. This style of memory tends to be easier to recall, because each item is connected to another important item, doubling the chances of the brain finding the information it needs. How many of the topics in your staff training are linked together, so that when your staff remember one concept, they automatically remember another important piece of information as well?

In many of his books and workshops, Michael Brandwein will use mnemonic devices to help staff remember key concepts. These, too, are examples of educational triggers. For example, WIBYT, stands for *write it before you talk*. The act of writing down information is a more engaged level of learning than just listening. Sometimes, in the act of writing down the concept being taught, a student (or staff member) will have sufficient time to consider the concept themselves, and draw their own conclusion, rather than jumping to ask additional questions. WIBYT isn't just a mnemonic device, it is a great idea that will encourage your staff to think more deeply about the information you are presenting.

■ Additional Hints, Suggestions, Ideas, Methods, Models, References and Tools

Here are a few more ideas for continuing to improve the environment of your staff-training sessions and to create a positive culture within your organization. Think of this as a list of opportunities, each one capable of improving the quality of your next staff training program.

For starters, get to know your local library. No doubt you have a very busy season ahead, and staff training is just one part of it. Before the season arrives, visit your local library or bookstore and invest some time reading the books mentioned in this section. Many of the books referenced in this book were borrowed from the local public library. You can also find quite a bit of information about these subjects on the Internet.

There are a variety of search engines available on the Internet. These suggestions will help you optimize your search of Internet resources. Type a word like *icebreakers* into any Internet search engine and you'll receive millions of 'hits.' You'll need to sift through each site to find the information you need. Instead, try typing *"icebreakers PDF"* (include the quotation marks), which will give you complete files, rather than individual activities, in portable document format that is ready to print and add to your staff training manual. Even better, visit www.pdf-search-engine.com and use this tool to search for complete documents on a wide variety of staff-related topics, including some that were created by organizations just like yours. You'll find dozens of useful PDF files here, including camp songs, brain gym activities, icebreakers, teambuilding games, and some very specific staff-training ideas.

In addition to searching via text on the Internet, you can search for images. For example, if you want to explore various themes for your program this coming season, go to Google.com and click on the "images" button in the upper-left-hand corner of the main Google search page, and a new page with Google Image Search will pop up. You can now enter any topic and photographs, illustrations, and graphics will appear. If you type in *scavenger hunt,* you'll not only obtain photographs of various types of scavenger hunts in progress, you'll also find scavenger hunt signs, posters and other unique graphics that will make your programs very colorful.

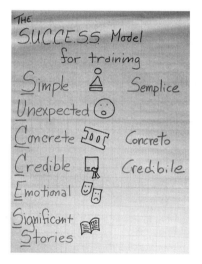

The book *Made to Stick—Why Some Ideas Survive & Others Die,* by Chip and Dan Heath (2007: ISBN 978-1-4000-6428-1), demonstrates a very simple model for ensuring that your students retain the information you share with them. The SUCCESS model presented in this book suggests that if you make your information: Simple, Unexpected, Concrete, Credible, Emotional and involve StorieS. By doing so, you'll provide the kind of learning environment where your staff will not only retain the information you present, but be able to use it in the future!

Research-Based Strategies to Ignite Student Learning: Insights from a Neurologist and Classroom Teacher, 2006, Judy Willis (ISBN 978-1416603702), provides a unique collection of advice from someone who is both a teacher and a neurologist.

For each different way you learn something, another memory pathway is created in the brain. Each pathway then becomes one more possible way you have of remembering and using that information. Think of it like this. The first time you learn the directions to a location, say a nearby hardware store, you tend to begin with landmarks that you already know, eventually venturing off to new routes. After you have driven these routes a few times, you find other ways of getting there—back roads, alternate routes, shortcuts. Now you have multiple ways of achieving the same goal, to get to the hardware store. So it is with learning something. The more pathways you have, the more opportunities you have for remembering. Or in the case of our example, actually arriving at the hardware store.

Paul Dennison's work in *Brain Gym* techniques is presented in several of his books, including *Brain Gym—Revised Teacher's Edition* by Paul and Gail Dennison (Ventura, CA: Edu-Kinesthetics, 1989, ISBN 0-942143-02-7). The idea that physical movement prepares the body and awakens the mind for learning is a concept that you can use during your staff trainings. Nearly every teacher, trainer, and facilitator has witnessed the drop in energy most audiences have after lunch. Brain gym techniques can reenergize and refocus your group.

Several of the activities in this book specifically use movement to build energy and engagement in the group. Try the *Story Stretch* or *Marching to the Beat of a Different Drum* the next time your staff begins to lose energy. You can also use many of the Brain Gym exercises to energize your staff.

One of the most recent books by Dennison about Brain Gym is *Brain Gym and Me: Reclaiming the Pleasure of Learning* (Ventura CA: Edu-Kinesthetics, Inc., 2006, ISBN 978-0942-143-11-9). Also, see the book *Smart Moves—Why Learning Is Not All in Your Head* by Carla Hannaford (1995, ISBN 0-915556-27-8) for even more ideas about the value of movement in active learning.

Tom Andrews has a very simple but profound teaching model that should be part of every organization's staff training creed. Tom shares the following information with the participants in each of his training workshops:

#1 I respect you.

#2 Because I respect you, I am going to share the very best knowledge, tools, information, activities, and techniques that I know.

#3 Because I respect you and share the best information that I know, I am going to hold you accountable to use this information to improve the world.

Tell your next staff this information before you begin training, and they'll be more likely to listen carefully to the content you present. In fact, Tom's model is a sure way to avoid the four fatal assumptions of Clarke and Crossland, presented next.

Although most of the models shared in this section are built on a positive theme to learning, education, and staff development, the following model is not. It concerns four fatal assumptions that can severely limit the effectiveness of your efforts to train and educate your staff. According to the work of Boyd Clarke and Ron Crossland in their book *The Leader's Voice—How Your Communication Can Inspire Action and Get Results* (ISBN 978-1590790168), effective leaders (teachers, directors, managers) communicate using three distinct techniques: facts, emotions, and symbols. Although these techniques are practical, useful, and even effective, devotion to only a single technique can minimize the overall effectiveness of the message being presented. Furthermore, Clarke and Crossland suggest that leaders make the following (typically fatal) assumptions about their audiences.

1. They understand the information being presented.
2. They agree with the information being presented.
3. They care about the information being presented.
4. They will act accordingly using this information.

Think about what you will need to do in your next staff training session to avoid these four fatal assumptions. How can you ensure that your audience is listening and that the information is getting through to them? How can you provide an open door policy so that any staff member can voice their concern or agreement with a particular rule or regulation of your organization? How can you get your staff to care enough to act on the information they have received?

Robert Fulghum's writings have inspired generations, and the following essays are especially inspirational as part of your staff training.

The Mermaid is specifically mentioned with regard to the activity *Shaping the Future* found in this book. *Yelling* is also worth reading with regard to customer service and working with individuals. Both of these essays can be found in the original and 15th anniversary editions of *All I Really Need to Know I Learned in Kindergarten* (ISBN 0-345-46617-9).

If you'd like some great opening conversation questions, read *The List*. For an inspirational closing reading, share *The Meaning of Life* (starting on page 290). Or better yet, listen to Robert Fulghum read this story himself, by using the book on CD for this same title. Both of these readings can be found in the book *What on Earth Have I Done?* (ISBN 0-312-36549-7).

Tom Rath's book *Vital Friends* (ISBN 1-59562-007-9) provides some very helpful numbers quantifying the effect that positive relationships have within a work group. This book is highly recommended. Many of the training activities presented in this book will assist you in the process of forming relationships and building a positive culture in your workplace.

Of the significant statistics presented by Rath, three are unforgettable. First, that teenagers (including those in your work force) spend nearly one-third of their time with friends, while the average for the rest of life is less than 10 percent. This number quantifies just how important relationships are to the youngest members of a work force. Second, 96 percent of employees with at least three close friends at work reported that they were *extremely satisfied* with their lives. Again, this shows the importance of relationships. Finally and most importantly, the percentage of engaged employees in the general work force is about 29 percent (with 54 percent disengaged and 17 percent actively disengaged). For employees without a friend at work, these numbers drop to 8 percent engaged, 63 percent disengaged, and 29 percent actively disengaged. But the good news is that for employees with a best friend at work, 56 percent are engaged! That is nearly double the average and a whopping eight times the engagement of those without friends in the workplace.

Visit www.vitalfriends.org for more information about this study, and the value of relationships in the workplace.

Harvey Downey, a facilitator from Great Britain, shared a story related to the success rate of recruits successfully passing the basic military training of the Royal Navy. When petty officers at HMS Raleigh in Cornwall were asked what significant factors made the difference between a recruit passing or failing basic training, one drill instructor remarked, "If a recruit can make friends here, or a borderline case can make even a single friend, they will probably make it through. If they do not make friends, no matter how promising they are, they will not make it!" Other instructors nodded in agreement.

The number-one factor for successfully passing basic training was to *make a friend* during the process. Those who were successful built positive relationships during their basic training period. Many of those who were unsuccessful did not build friendships during this stressful period.

Ask yourself, where in my staff-training program is there an opportunity for members of my staff to make a friend? If the answer is *nowhere,* you might want to reconsider the importance of this vital component.

One final model reinforces the need for building positive relationship in *any* organization. There are three significant components of a high-performing organization:

1. *The task is worth doing.* Habitat for Humanity is one example of an organization with a worthy task.
2. *There is a chance to grow and acquire new skills.* No matter what role you play in an organization, the opportunity to continue to learn is a valuable component.
3. *There is an opportunity to develop and maintain relationships in the workplace.*

If the organization you work for has all three of these vital components, the chances that you'll have a high quality work life, better staff retention, and higher overall job satisfaction, is very high. Most importantly, the lack of any one of these components is often attributed to an unsuccessful culture within an organization.

Think of these three ingredients as the ingredients to an organization pie. If you have all three necessary ingredients, in the right proportions, your pie tastes pretty good. But even if you have two outstanding ingredients, they will not make up for the lack of the third (necessary) ingredient. It is not enough any more to give your staff a great job to do, and some appropriate staff training to help them do it. You *absolutely* need to help them create positive relationships in the workplace.

If you feel that the culture of your organization could stand some improvement, ask yourself these questions. Which of the three components above is my organization missing? If I were to increase the amount of one of these components, which one would yield the greatest return and effect the greatest impact on my organization's culture? Is there any component that my organization is stressing, that is causing a negative shift in our culture?

If you don't happen to have any relationship-building plans for your next staff training session, have no fear. This book alone has more than a dozen useful activities for building positive relationships with your staff.

By the way, if you need to convince your board or superiors of the validity of building positive relationships during the staff-training process, here is a technique that builds on the stages of group development explored in this book and can actually assign a dollar value to what positive staff relationships are worth.

For most organizations, it is possible to calculate the salaries of all employees so that the cost of the entire organization can be known for any given day. As an example, let's consider an organization of 50 staff members, all new to the organization and all working on the same project. As this group progresses through the stages of group development (from forming to storming to norming to performing to transforming), they require different skills for each stage. The storming stage can be one of the least cost-effective (and most frustrating) stages of group development. By spending a bit more time in the forming stage (where positive staff relationships begin), it is possible to actually shorten the amount of time required for the group to pass through the storming stage, and move onto the norming and performing stages where real productivity and effort reside.

For every day your staff flounders in the storming stage, there is a cost to your organization. If you can shorten the total amount of time they stay in the storming process, you can save your organization some significant costs. If the cost of the 50 employees in our example was $10,000 per day, then the savings of a single day of storming behavior would be worth the same. If you can avoid the cost of one day of storming by providing the opportunity for building positive relationships in the forming stage (often at a cost much less than the salaries of your 50 employees), wouldn't it be worth it?

The National Longitudinal Study on Adolescent Health was designed to measure factors of risk and protection for youth, with over 12,000 adolescents interviewed. The very first result presented by Michael Resnick et al. in the *Journal of the American Medical Association* article on this study states that *"parent-family connectedness and perceived school connectedness were protective against every health risk behavior measured"* except one. Simply stated, if you want to protect youth in general and your youngest employees specifically, help them feel *connected* to the members of your team.

For more information on this study, read: "Protecting adolescents from harm: Findings from the National Longitudinal Study on Adolescent Health," Resnick, Bearman, Blum, Bauman, et al., *JAMA,* September 10, 1997, Volume 278, Issue 10, page 823–832.

If you want to evaluate the effectiveness of your staff-training program, read David Kirkpatrick's book, *Evaluating Training Programs—The Four Levels* (ISBN 978-1576753484). Chapter 19 on experiential and outdoor training was written by Richard Wagner, an outstanding educator and experiential learning specialist, now at the University of Wisconsin at Whitewater.

For one of the most interesting and recent books on training, read *Telling Ain't Training* by Harold Stolovitch and Erica Keeps (ISBN 978-1562863289). Of all the books we researched during the writing of this book, this one stood out for the variety of interesting training information shared. Here is one example of how the work of Stolovitch and Keeps and Michael Brandwein connect:

The information contained in your short-term memory begins to fade in about 20 seconds, and the number of informational chunks this memory can retrain is only five to nine independent pieces. Telephone numbers are seven digits long for a reason! If you can parcel information in your training sessions into connected chunks, rather than single pieces of information, your staff will have a much easier time remembering. Consider as an example Brandwein's use of mnemonics in the WIBYT example from the educational triggers section previously in this chapter. Write It Before You Talk, is five pieces of information, but WIBYT is just one. No wonder mnemonics are such a useful memory device!

Joanna Carolan's book *Little World—A Book about Tolerance* (ISBN 0-9715333-5-0) makes inspirational reading for your staff-training program. It is a perfect lead-in for discussion on diversity and tolerance. Which do you think is more likely in the next 10 years—that your community, work force, and staff will be more ethnically diverse, or less? For anyone answering "more," *Little World* is a good place to start.

The book *Everybody Needs a Rock* (ISBN 0-6897-1051-8) by Byrd Baylor and Peter Parnall, tells a great story about choosing the perfect rock for yourself. Read this one to your staff while standing near a riverbed with thousands of rocks all around. Although choosing the perfect rock may not be a specific goal of your next staff training session, this book does provide a great example of creating a sensory-rich learning environment. Ask several members of your staff to read a page or two of this book. Chances are, everyone will be engaged during this part of the program. And the rock they choose will become a life-long memento of this experience.

Edgar Dale's work using various presentation skills and measuring his student's retention of this information is an example of the power of multisensory learning tools. His *cone of learning* is often used to advocate using higher levels of activity to increase the retention of information in traditional learning environments. And while there is some controversy related to his model, it does have parallel significance with some more recent brain research that suggests creating multiple pathways in the brain (by teaching in a variety of ways). It improves retention and recollection of information.

Passive learning generally has a lower level of retention than more active techniques. Today, these active training techniques include song lyrics, videos (including DVDs, and Internet sources like youtube.com), graphics, music, movies, TV shows, stories, text messages, and even photographs from your cell phone. One resource, the *Teach with Movies* Web site *(www.teachwithmovies.com),* shows how recent and classic movie clips can be used to reinforce training topics. If you use computer-generated slideshows, there is a slideshow sharing Web site *(www.slideshare.net)* where you can find hundreds of training themes and slideshows, including one of the more interesting global awareness slideshows, Shift Happens:

> *The ability to grasp and retain new information, skills, and tools is a direct response to the environment where learning takes place. The greater the stimulation and immersion of the student in the learning process, the greater the retention, recollection, and application of the information.*

Marcia Tate's work related to brain research and growing dendrites through active learning is presented in her article in the January/February 2006 issue of the American Camp Association's *Camping* magazine, and also in her 2004 book *"Sit and Get" Won't Grow Dendrites: 20 Professional Learning Strategies That Engage the Adult Brain.* In this article, Marcia mentions 20 strategies for improving the learning process, including facilitation instead of teaching, creative and artistic expression, field trips, games, graphics, humor, haptic (tactile) objects, metaphors, movement, music, drama, storytelling, technology, visual aids, and journaling.

For more staff-training-friendly brain research ideas from Marcia, you'll find a list of her books in the references section of this book.

▥ H.A.L.T.

The following model was shared by a staff member of a peer counseling organization. It is valuable information indeed, and worth considering when training your staff.

If you are *hungry, angry, lonely* or *tired,* it is time for a break. Trying to push a group or an individual through any one of these situations has a diminishing return on your investment. It is far better to take a break, rectify the issue at hand, and then return to the discussion or topic at a later time.

During any staff training program, there generally comes a time when the energy of the group drops. Be aware of this probability, and have a strategy ready. As an example, from this book, try using an energizer (such as the *Leadership Dance*) to reinvigorate your audience, before continuing your staff training agenda.

Be Here Now!

YUM, the corporation that coordinates Pepsi's restaurants (like Taco Bell, KFC, and Pizza Hut), has a great poster in nearly every one of its conference/training rooms. It simple says, "Be here now!"

In the next year, the number of staff members arriving with music earphones in their ears and text-messaging devices switched on during your training sessions will no doubt increase, unless you make a concerted effort to help them be fully present during the training process. You're going to need to show them the culture of what happens in your organization, and the appropriate place and time for these devices. You might consider your own "Be here now!" campaign.

The Competency Ladder

Before you begin teaching your staff any concept, consider the following ladder model. Each step of this model signifies an increase in the skill level of the participant. The higher the level, the greater the ability of the student to successfully utilize the knowledge gained. You should ask yourself before you begin writing your teaching plan, "*What level do I want my staff to achieve as a result of my teaching?*" If it is acceptable for your staff to have a basic awareness of a concept (e.g., staff should park their cars in the parking area behind the maintenance building), then you probably can move quickly through this information and expect that most of your staff will park their vehicles appropriately.

Mastery
Proficiency
Competency
Knowledge
Awareness

If, however, you need your staff to exhibit a high level of mastery on a particular subject (moving campers to a safe location in the event of high winds, which are likely to occur later this week), then as an instructor, teacher, and facilitator, you need to use educational techniques that will move your staff beyond simple awareness and knowledge, and well into competent and perhaps even mastery (perfection) of this particular piece of knowledge. Concepts that demand mastery from your staff require mastery in their presentation to your staff.

The concept of *see one, do one, teach one* from earlier in this chapter is applicable here as well. *Each one teach one* is another way of expressing this same philosophy.

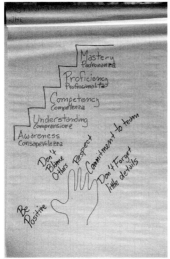

Students move up the competency ladder when they are presented with a new concept (awareness), given the opportunity to explore and practice this concept (knowledge and competency), and allowed to perfect their ability to the point where they are able to share this knowledge with others (proficiency and mastery). So if you want mastery from your staff on a particular subject, be sure your teaching presentation mirrors this level of ability and allows the opportunity for the student to perfect their abilities, not merely observe the subject.

In a similar fashion to the competency ladder, the target model can help a trainer plan the appropriate amount of content to actually deliver the necessary outcomes to an organization. Several facilitators and trainers have mentioned that they were considered failures by organizations for not delivering cultural change (and group behavioral changes), even though these same organizations rejected their proposals for sufficient time, resources, and curriculum latitude to actually effect such changes. Many organizations want such culture shifting behavior in their work teams, but few fully understand the level of training actually necessary to accomplish it.

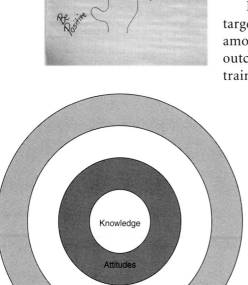

Consider the target model shown here. The amount of time, curriculum, effort, and indeed difficulty encountered to effect changes in the concepts noted in each ring increases as you move further outward from the center. Like the competency ladder, basic knowledge is achievable with a limited investment. For higher levels of competency, additional effort is required. In the case of this target model, the greater the magnitude of change required, the greater the difficulty in accomplishing such a change. Don't make the mistake of trying to change the group behavior of an entire staff, in 20 minutes of lecture.

The Six Rs

In her office, Clare-Marie Hannon has a small sign with the six Rs. Make sure when you tell your staff about specific rules and regulations in your organization, you also tell

---

them why these are necessary, and why these are nonnegotiables. Simply stated, if you create rules and regulations without reasons and respect, you'll get resentment and rebellion from your staff.

$$\frac{\textbf{(Rules + Regulations)} - \textbf{(Reasons + Respect)}}{\textbf{(Resentment + Rebellion)}}$$

The works of M. J. Ellis, Yerkes, and Dodson, and others have explored the theme of *optimal arousal* or peak learning. Simply stated, students achieve the highest levels of interest in learning when the ratio of the skills they possess and the skills they are presented to learn are at an optimal ratio. If their interest level is too low (i.e., they cannot see the application or need for the subject matter), their ability to retain and utilize the information is minimized. The more optimal their interest level, the more likely they will retain and apply the information they receive. There is an upper limit, as well. Too high an arousal level, and students are unable to focus. The optimal arousal model is often referred to as the Yerkes-Dodson principle or the inverted-U theory, and relates arousal level to performance. Sports psychologists have used the optimal arousal theory for achieving high performance in athletes. And by optimal, they do not mean maximum arousal. Rather, the goal is the optimum level of arousal (focus, intensity, readiness) for the situation.

Think for yourself, from past staff-training experiences: When was your audience most interested, focused, and ready to learn? Keep a journal this coming year, and make notes after each specific section of your staff training program. Mark which training topics could use a boost in student focus, and which ones are just fine. Use some of the activities and methods in this book to improve the staff training topics that you decide need higher student involvement.

Mihaly Csikszentmihalyi's research on *flow* (the sweet spot between boredom and anxiety) is another way of expressing this same phenomena, and not surprisingly, it also has a sports psychology component. When you provide an atmosphere of learning that moves beyond boredom for students and does not exceed the level that would cause anxiety, you will have achieved the optimal learning environment. Most students don't consciously realize that they are in flow until after they have left it again. "Wow, I was really focused back there, wasn't I?"

For more reading on this subject, try an Internet search using keywords such as *optimal arousal learning* or *Yerkes-Dodson Principle*. You can also read *Finding Flow,* by Mihaly Csikszentmihalyi, 1977 Basic Books, New York, or *Beyond Boredom and Anxiety* by the same author.

There are no shortcuts to any place worth going.
—Beverly Sills

The strength of the United States is not the gold at Fort Knox or the weapons of mass destruction that we have, but the sum total of the education and the character of our people.
—Claiborne Pell (1918–2009)

Education is not the filling of a pail, but the lighting of a fire.
—William Butler Yeats (1865–1939)

The great aim of education is not knowledge but action.
—Herbert Spencer

Planning and Making the Most of Essential Staff Training Activities

2

Here is a list of all the activities presented in this book and advice for making the most of each of them. As many facilitators and trainers know, any activity can be modified to explore different themes and teachable moments. For simplicity in both this listing and the detailed explanation of each activity, we have chosen to present the most staff-training-appropriate theme. But just remember, there are limitless possibilities for using these activities to benefit your staff, now and in the future.

The Top Ten Staff Training Activities—The Best of the Best

If you have time for only a few activities in your staff training plans, start with these!

TABLE 2.1

No.	Activity Name	Teachable Moment	Equipment Required
1.	The Story of Your Name	Respect, name memory	None
2.	First Impressions	Avoiding stereotypes	Paper/pencil
3.	Over Here!	Inclusion, acceptance	Raccoon circles
4.	Celebration	Enthusiasm, connection	None
5.	The Blind Trust Drive	Trust building	None
6.	Four Corners	Connection, choice	None
7.	Quotes in Order	Mission, memory	Index cards, markers
8.	Character Cards	Discussing character	Character cards
9.	Bull Ring Candelabra	Teamwork, unity	Bull rings, PVC tubes
10.	A Circle of Connection	Unity, connection	None

Thirty More Staff Training Activities

Here are thirty more activities that explore an even wider range of staff training topics, plus a special bonus leadership activity.

TABLE 2.2

No.	Activity Name	Teachable Moment	Equipment Required
11.	Handshakes	Face Recognition, Connect	None
12.	Walk and Talk	Finding common ground	None
13.	Wrapped Around My Finger	History giving, sharing	Raccoon Circle
14.	Autographs	Exploring TGR model	Papers/Pens
15.	The Big Question	Conversation, icebreaker	Index Cards
16.	The Big Answer	Advice and Assistance	Papers/Pens
17.	Leadership Dance	Leadership, Energizer	Music
18.	Pieces of a Puzzle	Group Problem Solving	Paper
19.	Arrowheads	Managing Resources	Arrowhead Puzzles
20.	Not Knots	Consensus, Failing Forward	Short Rope
21.	The Change Train	Coaching, Change	None
22.	Petecas	Change, Creative Twists	Petecas
23.	Pop It	Understanding Roles and Rules	Balloons
24.	Inside Out	Problem solving, ethics	Raccoon Circles
25.	Tie the Knot	Problem solving, teamwork	Short Ropes
26.	Finding Your Place	Unity, belonging	Wood Shapes
27.	Magic Carpet	Problem solving, goals	Tarps
28.	The Helium Stick	Group problem solving	Lightweight Tube
29.	Alphabet Soup	Group problem solving	Index Cards, Rope
30.	The PVC Network	Problem solving, teamwork	Teamplay Tubes
31.	Wah!	Energizer games, fun	None
32.	Nose Jousting	Sportsmanship, energizer	Masking Tape
33.	Interference	Communication	Ball, Rope Lines
34.	Object Retrieval	Multiple solutions, planning	Ropes and more
35.	Texas Leghorn	Aerobic energizer, fun	Rubber Chicken
36.	Vision Walk	Creating a common vision	Bandanas
37.	Playing Card Line Up	Knowing where you fit	Playing Cards
38.	Hieroglyphics	Linguistic problem solving	Puzzle Pages
39.	Loop the Loop	Adaptation and change	Raccoon Circles
40.	Stretching the Limit	Planning, time management	Misc. Props
41.	$10 \times 10 \times 10$ (Bonus!)	Leadership and teamwork	Boards and Ropes

▰ Ten Activities to Help Your Staff Navigate the Stages of Group Development

Two activities for each of the five stages of group development. These activities are active, engaging, fun, and they require minimal props.

TABLE 2.3

No.	Activity Name	Teachable Moment	Equipment Required	Stage
42.	Believe It or Knot	Get-acquainted activity	Raccoon Circle	Forming
43.	Where Ya From	History giving	Raccoon Circle	Forming
44.	Cross the Line	Conflict Resolution	Raccoon Circle	Storming
45.	People Movers	Overcoming Adversity	Sheets of Paper	Storming
46.	The Missing Link	Consensus Building	Raccoon Circles	Norming
47.	Eagle in the Wind	Trust Building	None	Norming
48.	Grand Prix Racing	Teamwork, Enthusiasm	Raccoon Circle	Performing
49.	Sunny Side Up	Team Challenge	Tarp and Ball	Performing
50.	A Circle of Kindness	Closure, Connection	None	Transforming
51.	The Four Minute Team	Problem Solving, Unity	None	Transforming

▰ Creative Presentation Techniques

This is an introduction to techniques and methods for improving your presentation of the activities in this book.

TABLE 2.4

No.	Activity Name	Teachable Moment	Equipment Required
52.	River Crossing	Team problem solving	Stepping stones (carpet squares)
53.	How's the Weather Cards	Framing the Experience	Story Cards
54.	Team Performance Cards	Visual Team Behaviors	Team Performance Cards
55.	Virtual Slideshow	Unique debriefing method	Clicker
56.	Tunes	A musical challenge	Spoons, water, glasses

Ready-to-Copy Pages

This chapter contains pages that can be copied and used for the activities listed. You are welcome to make copies of these pages for your staff training programs.

TABLE 2.5

No.	Activity Name	Teachable Moment	Equipment Required
2.	First Impressions	Avoiding Stereotypes	Paper/pencil
8.	Character Cards	Discussing Character	Character cards
14.	Autographs	Exploring TGR Model	Paper/pens
15.	The Big Question	Conversation, Icebreaker	Index cards
16.	The Big Answer	Advice and Assistance	Paper/pens
18.	Pieces of a Puzzle	Group Problem Solving	Paper
19.	Arrowhead Puzzle Profile	Managing Resources	Arrowhead puzzles
24.	Problem Solving Cards	Nine-step solution model	Raccoon circles
30.	The PVC Network	Problem solving, teamwork	Teamplay tubes
38.	Hieroglyphics	Linguistic problem solving	Puzzle pages
41.	$10 \times 10 \times 10$ Script	Leadership and teamwork	Boards and ropes
53.	How's the Weather Cards	Visual group assessment	Story cards
54.	Team Performance Cards	Visual team performance	Team performance cards

The Top Ten Staff Training Activities
The Best of the Best

There is a very good reason why these first ten activities have a chapter all to themselves. If you have a full training schedule and you only have time for a few activities, then we recommend that you choose from these first ten activities. The authors have used all these activities during staff-training programs, with great success. You can, too.

1. The Story of Your Name

Here is one of the best activities for creating a culture of respect in any organization. This activity is especially valuable if you happen to have considerable diversity in your staff.

We all have a story related to our name. Some of us are named after another member of our family, a close friend of our parents, or perhaps someone famous. Many men and women know what their name would have been, had they been born the opposite gender. Our middle names are significant, too. For this activity, invite all participants to share the story of their name. How did they come to have it? Do they

like it? Who else has their name? What nicknames do they have? Encourage them to end with the phrase, "Please call me. . . . *their name of choice here.*" In this way, everyone will have the opportunity to say how they would like to be addressed, and what is positive about their name. A very powerful activity indeed.

Although this activity requires no equipment, it does require significant time. Most participants speak for a minute or two. That means if you have 30 staff members, you can easily spend an hour with this one activity. It is time well spent, given that all your staff will know how to address each other, and are much more likely to remember not only each other's names, but the stories behind them as well.

At a technical conference at Penn State University, I met several graduate students from other universities. One student from China had arrived in the United States only two days earlier, and her language skills were challenging. But we did manage to introduce her to ice cream from the on-campus ice cream store, which quickly became her favorite American food.

At dinner, she introduced herself to our group, and her name was very unusual. It was not a name that I found familiar or easy to pronounce. When I asked her what her name meant, she mentioned that everyone in her family had great names. "My name means 'all the colors of the rainbow' in my native language," she said. "What does your name mean?"

What followed was a lengthy introduction by all the members of our group, telling us all the interesting facts, stories, and unusual consequences of their names. And best of all, these stories made it very easy to remember everyone's name throughout the conference.

Jim Cain

Notes

2. First Impressions

First Impressions is a terrific activity for challenging your staff to go beyond their first impressions with other staff members. It challenges stereotypes. It encourages participants to go beyond appearance. It makes it easy for new staff members to talk to each other, and best of all, the final question connects the members of your staff together! If you explore Daniel Goleman's book, *Social Intelligence*, you'll find that First Impressions is an excellent activity for beginning the process of social awareness and making valuable connections that will last.

In groups of three, provide each of your staff members with a copy of the First Impressions activity page and a pencil or pen. You can find a full-size version of this activity in the Ready-to-Copy section of this book. Encourage each group to include other staff members that they don't know very well (yet). Within each group, each person guesses each of the traits about the two partners. This is not a conversation (yet). Each person just makes a best guess and writes this guess in the outer margins of the page (on the left, for the person sitting on their left, and on the right for the person sitting on their right). When all three participants have finished guessing each of the traits on their sheet, it is time for first sharing their guesses, and then having each person share their true story about each of these items. Encourage your staff to keep track of how many traits they guessed correctly.

This activity begins very quietly, as each participant studies their partners and guesses each of the traits listed on their paper. As your staff begin to share their guesses, moderate volume begins, followed by occasional outbreaks of laughter, giggling, and other exclamations as guesses and correct answers are revealed.

Groups generally do not finish in exactly the same time, but fortunately, this activity encourages conversation between the members of each group, so even after finishing First Impressions groups continue talking about all sorts of useful things.

The final question in this activity (What do you have in common with this person?) is a wonderful way for your staff to start seeing other members of the staff for what they share in common, rather than focusing on what is different about them. If you would like to alter some of the questions, here are a few ideas, or make up your own staff specific questions.

1. Where would they go on vacation? (mountains, ocean, big city, overseas, etc.)
2. What kinds of vehicle do they drive?
3. What would they do with fifty dollars?
4. What is their favorite book of all time?
5. What order in their family are they? (oldest, middle, youngest)
6. What can you tell about this person by the shoes they are wearing?

BOX 3.2

The summer camp staff for one camp near Harrisonburg, Virginia, had two members from Australia. One member of the staff remarked, "Oh you're from Australia. You must eat vegemite." To which both Australian staff members said (almost in unison), "No, we never eat it! Why do people assume that all Australians eat vegemite?"

As our world continues to diversify, you'll have staff members that do not look like the other members of your staff. Age, height, appearance, ethnicity, gender, physical skills, language, tattoos, smoking preferences—these are all examples of how your new staff can vary from your last staff. Be prepared to explore this diversity. First Impressions is a kind way to begin this process.

Notes

3. Over Here!

This simple activity can increase the inclusiveness of any organization. From the classroom to the boardroom, this activity encourages participants to openly invite others to join them, in a friendly and boisterous manner.

Begin by spreading several knotted Raccoon Circles around the floor space. You'll need one circle for every six people. Invite everyone in your staff to stand inside one of these circles.

> *"I'm going to invite you to learn a little about the people in your circle. Let's start with an easy one; point to the person in your group that is the tallest. When I say, 'one, two, three,' you wave goodbye to this person and say 'see ya!' Once this person leaves your circle, they become a free agent. But your group has lost a person. The way to invite someone to join your circle is to yell, 'over here, over here!'*
>
> *Now, here are a few ground rules. Is it ok to get the same person back? Yes it is! Is it ok to get more than one person? Sure. Can you go out and recruit new members? Yes. Do you know the difference between recruitment and abduction? Recruitment is noncontact!"*

Once your staff understand the basic rules, you can begin the activity with some of the categories shown as follows. The *free agent* can be invited to any group. Some groups will soon overflow their circle boundary. Other groups may soon lose all of their members. Some groups on the outside perimeter may choose to move their circle to a "better location." Lots of strategies are possible here.

Who has the most books in their personal library?
Who has watched the most videos this month?
Who has traveled the farthest distance from here?
Who has the most unused fitness equipment?
Who has the most unusual middle name?
Who has the most brothers and sisters?
Who is wearing the coolest watch?
Who is wearing the most jewelry?
Who has the shortest hair?
Who is the youngest?
Who is the tallest?

In addition to the category for identifying the free agent, you can ask another question to each group for conversation purposes:

Who has visited the most countries?
Who collects something interesting?
Who was born in a foreign country?
Who delivered newspapers as a kid?
Who has the oldest living relative?
Who speaks the most languages?
Who owns the most pets?
Who has acted on stage?

Don't underestimate the power of this simple activity. By creating a situation where your staff members feel comfortable joining *any* group of fellow staff members, you can avoid some of the traditional separation that can occur between various segments of your staff. In some summer camps, for example, it is not uncommon for program staff and counselors to each form their own clique. If you include Over Here! in your staff training program, you'll continue to hear your staff saying, "over here, over here," to invite others to join them.

Thanks to Chris Cavert for allowing us to share this excellent get-acquainted activity, which he calls See Ya. You can find out more about Chris, his books, and his work at www.fundoing.com.

BOX 3.3

While working with several classrooms of elementary students one day, I managed to become separated from the other teachers and adults during the lunchtime period. After joining the students in the lunch line, I stood at the cafeteria door looking for any sign of the grown-ups. Seeing me looking for a seat, one of the students from my morning session stood up on his chair, waved his arms and yelled, "Over here, over here!" Suddenly, I had a place to go where I was wanted! I never even looked for the rest of the grown-ups. I ate lunch with "my people."

Most students will tell you that lunchtime in any high school is one of the most segregated times in our modern culture. Students instinctively know where they are welcome and where they are not. The simple act of one student inviting me to sit with him and his friends created a very inclusive atmosphere.

If you choose to use this activity with your staff, don't be surprised if occasionally (during lunch or a staff meeting) you hear someone yell, "Over here, over here!"

Jim Cain

▪ 4. Celebration

No matter how much energy you put into your training program, there is sure to be a time when you'd like to reenergize your staff. Here is a great activity that will continue to energize your staff long after it's first introduced. And best of all, it requires no equipment at all.

Begin with a quick discussion of how important it is to celebrate both big and small successes with your staff. Invite your staff to talk about the successes they expect to share while working together. What kinds of things count as big successes? What small successes also need to be celebrated, so that they are not overlooked?

Next, invite everyone to find a partner and to create a unique *handshake.* Encourage creativity and invite a few partners to demonstrate their handshakes. With this same partner, they also create their own *high-five* movement. Again, ask for a few volunteers to demonstrate their technique. And finally, ask partners to create a *celebration dance.*

Designate one member of the group, such as the group leader, to initiate celebrations. Whenever they shout, "Celebrate!" everybody finds their partner, shakes hands, does a high-five, and finishes the celebration with their own unique dance movement.

Team celebrations mirror the energy with which the word *celebrate* is spoken, whispered, or shouted. A whispered "celebration" initiates a quiet series of movements. A shout is sure to unleash a wild and boisterous response.

During future and sometimes lengthy training sessions, a well-timed celebration can quickly transform uninspired individuals back into a laughing, energized team.

BOX 3.4

The camp director of Camp Icaros in Mexico, Francisco Labiaga (or Paco, as he likes to be called), created his own version of this activity, which he calls *the magic circle*. He uses this activity to reinforce the connection of his entire summer camp staff. During the summer, even campers are included in this fun ritual. As a closing activity, Paco includes music (*The Lion Sleeps Tonight* is his favorite).

At any time of the day, and especially when the group most needs it, someone calls out "*magic circle*," and everyone completes this ritual with three different partners:

Partners touch right fists and then left fists. Partners touch right elbows together, and then left elbows. Partners touch right shoulders and then left shoulders. Partners touch foreheads together and make eye contact and smile!

After three connections, everyone gathers in a big circle and awaits instruction for where to go next.

Notes

Stop worrying about the potholes in the road and celebrate the journey!
—Barbara Hoffman

📼 5. The Blind Trust Drive

Although there are many trust-building techniques, this unique activity is one of the finest for beginning the process of building trust within a group.

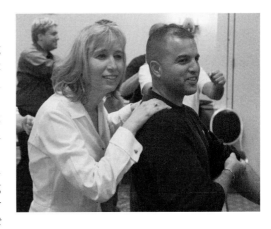

No equipment is required for this activity; however, you should conduct this activity in a large, flat area free of obstacles.

Begin with partners of similar heights, with one partner standing behind the other, both facing forward. The front *driver* holds onto an imaginary steering wheel and closes their eyes. The *'backseat driver'* has perfect vision, places their hands on the driver's shoulders and tells them, "Don't worry, I am going to make sure you are safe." The front driver controls the speed, while the rear driver provides information and direction, keeping both participants safe in the process. After a few minutes, the front driver opens their eyes and provides some feedback to the backseat driver on their technique. Next, the two participants exchange roles, after which another feedback session is provided.

This is an excellent activity for beginning a more in-depth trust sequence. Be sure to have plenty of supervision and a safe, flat area for this activity. Invite the initially blind drivers to provide the following feedback to their sighted partners: (1) What was good about their technique? (2) What could they have done to be even better?

On the front cover of Stephen M. R. Covey's book, *The Speed of Trust,* the phrase "trust is the one thing that changes everything!" appears. What better way to begin the process of your staff coming together and working together, than to build trust from the very beginning?

BOX
3.5

For this activity, I typically share a story about the staff director, which goes like this:

Imagine if you will that before today's staff-training session, you received a call from *(your director's name here)*. They asked you to stop by the store and pick up a few last-minute items for today's program, and they toss you the keys to their brand new car. And it is a very cool car indeed. The bad news is that today's weather is very unusual. It is foggy. So foggy, in fact, that you (front seat driver) can't see a thing. Close your eyes.

Luckily, this car has GPS navigation, so, backseat driver, you can see everything. Place your hands on the shoulders of the person in front of you, lean forward, say this (and mean it), "Don't worry, I'm going to take care of you!"

Notice that the tone of your statement does quite a bit to either help your front-seat driver feel comfortable or not. This is not bumper cars (dodge 'em cars, in the United Kingdom). This is not a demolition derby. Our goal today is zero contact with other drivers or fixed obstacles. And why do you want to be a great backseat driver? Because halfway through, when I say, "Switch places!" your backseat driver is going to remember just how good you were.

Backseat driver, just say to your front seat partner, "I've got your back!" Start your engines. Off you go!

Jim Cain

6. Four Corners (Discussion Squares)

When preparing your staff for work, it is important that they each understand their potential for influencing the minds of other staff members, customers, and associates. In the case of camp counselors, teachers, and other youth development leaders, this can mean influence of a potentially positive or negative quality in the lives of a young person. The more your staff understand how they interact with others, the more prepared they will be to act intentionally and with a positive effect.

Four Corners is an effective and nonthreatening activity that encourages discussion about experiences that have shaped who we are and how we interact with others. With regards to your staff-training program, Four Corners leads your staff through a process of thinking about the following:

- Who I am
- How I got here
- How I interact with people
- The style I want to develop

You won't need a significant amount of equipment to lead this activity. You'll just need to create four lines (with an unknotted Raccoon Circle, short segments of rope, masking tape, or sidewalk chalk) or four zones (with activity cones, chairs, or rope circles). Labeling each quadrant of the area or each zone is a nice touch, but not absolutely required. You'll also need a list of questions or topics that you would like to explore with your staff. You'll find a list of potential question sources at the end of this activity description.

Begin by posing a question to the group, and then asking each person to relocate to the corner that best represents their answer. Allow a few minutes for each group to discuss why they have made this choice and to share experiences. "*Why are you 'Cheez Whiz'?*" sounds like a silly question, but in this context it may lead to significant insights. After a few minutes, invite a representative from each square to share a few comments about their discussion.

Here are a few interesting topics that you can consider with your staff:

1. Which best describes your personality?

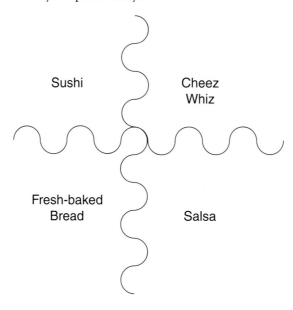

Sushi

Cheez
Whiz

Fresh-baked
Bread

Salsa

2. Think of the most significant adults in your life as you were growing up. Which style did you see the most?

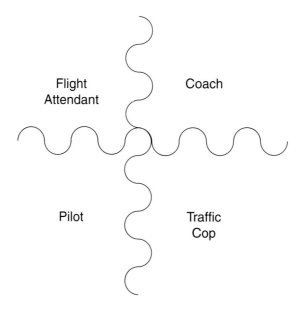

Flight
Attendant

Coach

Pilot

Traffic
Cop

3. Which best describes your leadership style?

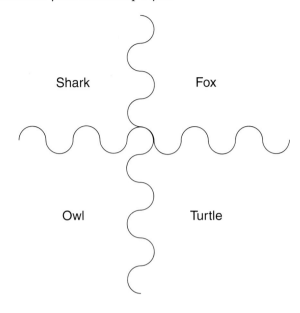

Shark   Fox

Owl   Turtle

4. Which best describes how you approach conflicts?

5. What best represents the style you want to develop?

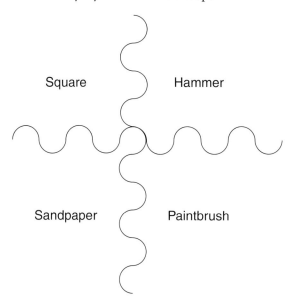

Square   Hammer

Sandpaper   Paintbrush

Consider following this activity with a period of quiet reflection and an opportunity to do some unstructured journaling. This process can lead to some significant personal insights. Four Corners can be an excellent lead-in to setting personal goals for improving interactions with the people we work with.

Variations

If four choices are too many for your staff, consider using three large circles and designate these as three possible answer choices. Next, ask your group a series of questions and invite them to move to the circle that best reflects their choice. For example, the question, *"Which of the following technologies is the best for communicating critical issues with the rest of the team?"* can have the

following three choices: (A) e-mail, (B) voicemail, (C) in person. Once groups have formed in each circle, encourage them to discuss their choice and reinforce why they made this particular choice.

And, if you really want to limit the possibilities, you can use a single rope to divide your space and only provide your staff with two choices, A or B (left side or right side).

BOX 3.6

You'll find more choice activities like these in *The Revised and Expanded Book of Raccoon Circles,* from authors Jim Cain and Tom Smith, 2007, Kendall/Hunt Publishers, ISBN 0-7575-3265-9. You can also find a wide variety of interesting questions in the following books:

The Book of Questions, 1987, Gregory Stock, Workman Publishing, New York, NY USA, ISBN 0-89480-320-4

The Book of Questions: Business, Politics and Ethics, 1991, Gregory Stock, Workman Publishing, New York, NY USA, ISBN 0-56305-034-X

If . . . (Questions for the Game of Life), 1995, Evelyn McFarlance & James Saywell, Villard Books, New York, NY USA, ISBN 0-679-44535-8

Think Twice – An Entertaining Collection of Choices, 1998, Bret Nicholaus and Paul Lowrie, Ballantine Books, New York, NY USA, ISBN 0-345-41759-3

The Conversation Pie – Creative Questions to Tickle the Mind, 1996, Bret Nicholaus and Paul Lowrie, Ballantine Books, New York, NY USA, ISBN 0-345-40711-3

You Gotta Be Kidding!, Randy Horn, Stephanie Ring and Marissa Fierz, 2006, Workman Publishing, New York, NY USA, ISBN 978-0761-14365-9

Notes

▬ 7. Quotes in Order

If you really want your staff to remember a critical piece of information, this activity will help them retain the message. Although the title uses the word *quotes,* this activity can help your staff memorize any short written phrase, such as a mission statement, vision statement, emergency situation response, or other vital and useful pieces of information.

Begin by choosing a quotation (or short phrase) for your staff to learn. You can find dozens of Web sites with searchable databases of quotations, including some in foreign languages; www.quotationspage.com is one example. This activity is most useful if your staff have not yet heard or seen the quotation or phrase you plan to present. In other words, use this activity to introduce a quotation or concept, not after you have already shared it with your staff.

Using blank index cards, write down one, two, or three words per card, until you have completed the quotation, including the author's name. A brief collection of several useful quotations are shown at the end of this activity description (including the example shown here). The quotation shown here contains sufficient cards to challenge a group of sixteen participants.

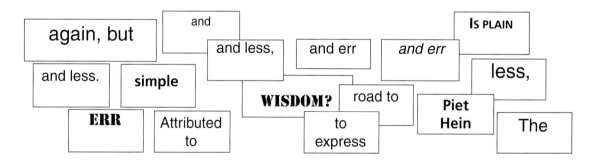

Next, randomly pass out one card per participant. Invite each person to hold their card so that others can easily read it, but remind participants not to give up their card.

The challenge is now for the group to successfully place themselves in a circle so that the quotation reads correctly from beginning to end.

Interestingly, some groups mimic the stages of group development with this one activity. Some general *forming* begins as members of the group first begin to speak. Politeness, openness, and searching for meaning are all present. Next, of course is the *storming* stage, as the group accepts some problem-solving techniques, but terminates others. Eventually, the group begins to create meaning from these randomly distributed cards, and reaches the *performing* stage of group development.

Participants are asked not to give up their cards during this activity. The reason for this restriction is to keep everyone in the group engaged. Participants who give up their cards (so that others can move them about, perhaps on the floor or a table), become spectators rather than participants.

As an aid to your staff, you can provide clues to assist them with this challenge. For the quote just shown, one of the most reasonable clues is for the group to identify who wrote this quotation. Piet Hein is not a North American name, and hence the group should not expect North American sentence structure. Capitalization may or may not work, but punctuation does (in this particular example). Similar words go together. And finally, upon the request of the group, the facilitator is willing to place any two people that the group selects into their correct positions. Again, all these aids are offered to assist the group in completing the task, not in providing the answer for them.

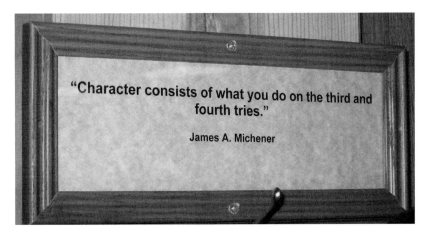

Here are a few interesting quotes that we have found:

Men wanted for hazardous journey. Small wages, bitter cold, long months of complete darkness, constant danger, safe return doubtful. Honour and recognition in case of success.
—Sir Ernest Shackleton
   Advertisement in London Newspaper, 1906 (some believe this quote is fictitious)

The great aim of education is not knowledge but action.
—Herbert Spencer (1820–1903)

The highest result of education is tolerance.
—Helen Keller (1880–1968)

The road to Wisdom? Is plain and simple to express—
Err, and err and err again, but less, and less and less.
—Piet Hein

The strength of the United States is not the gold at Fort Knox or the weapons of mass destruction
that we have, but the sum total of the education and the character of our people.
—Claiborne Pell (1918–)

Education is not the filling of a pail, but the lighting of a fire.
—W. B. Yeats

Active learning activities create an experience that opens the door for a meaningful conversation
about things that matter.
—Jim Cain

BOX 3.7

As mentioned in Chapter 1, this activity bridges the gap between short-term and long-term memory. By requiring a few minutes for the group to successfully place random words into a coherent and meaningful order, each participant internally processes the entire message until it is completed. When the complete quote makes sense, the brain can store this information more easily than a random series of words. Helping your staff make sense of specific information, rules, regulations, and procedures is part of this same process. At the completion of the activity, most group members will be able to articulate the exact message completely, without looking at the individual index cards.

Notes

⬛ 8. Character Cards

Here is an energetic card game that can be used to teach almost anything! The example shown here has the theme of character. You'll find picture cards of this topic in the ready-to-copy section of this book. For your staff training, you can choose to use this activity to introduce *any* subject, theme, or content to your staff.

To begin, you'll need twenty-four large index cards for each team of six to twelve participants. Write the same word, phrase, title, or illustration on two cards. You'll need twelve words or phrases for each deck of cards. Next, shuffle the cards to randomize their order. Then place them face down in a rectangular 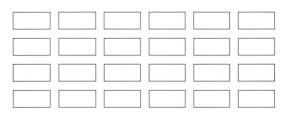 pattern about 10 to 15 feet (3 to 5 meters) from their team. Use an unknotted Raccoon Circle, short piece of rope, masking tape, or sidewalk chalk to create a starting line.

One person from each group is allowed to cross the line at a time. This person approaches the cards and is allowed to turn over any two cards. If the cards match, they are left turned face up. If the cards do not match, this person can show them to the teammates, but then must place them face down in their original position and step back. Then the next person from their team takes a turn. The first team to successfully turn over all twenty four cards wins the round.

Allow the teams two minutes to plan their strategy and the order in which team members will participate. The energy of this activity builds as each group nears completion. Some competition between groups is valuable here. Encourage cheering and teamwork.

Although this activity can be used to introduce your staff to any concepts in your training program, the real value comes after all the cards have been turned over. Here are several techniques you can use to create a powerful discussion with this activity:

1. Invite the members of the group to choose one card that they believe has a significant word or phrase. Ask each person to tell the group why they chose this card and why this concept is important to them.

2. Ask each group to decide as a team which five words are the most important from all the words shown. Compare these five words with the words chosen by members of the other teams. Discuss which words each team has in common and why they chose any unique words.

3. Ask your entire staff to focus on just one word. Which one do they feel is the single most important concept or word?

BOX 3.8

As part of a quarterly teambuilding day, one corporation (with a very stressful work environment) performed the Match Game as part of its program. During the debriefing portion of the activity, one participant chose the *respect* card, and mentioned that they didn't feel much of this characteristic in their workplace. What followed was a very honest and frank discussion by the entire group concerning the kinds of values, beliefs, characteristics, and behaviors they would ideally like to see in their work environment. This simple five-minute activity lead to an hour-long discussion that significantly altered and improved the working relationships of that corporate team. Don't underestimate the power of discussing character with each of the members of your own team!

For a large format double-deck of character cards printed in full color, contact Creative Concepts at: www.GivaGeta.com or (860) 657-0770. With this deck of fifty-eight cards, you can facilitate eleven different icebreakers, teambuilding challenges, and character-building activities. You can also purchase this product from Training Wheels, Inc.

9. Bull Ring Candelabra

Here is a variation of the teambuilding activity Bull Ring that will bring your entire staff together, and will leave them cheering at the finish! A bull ring is a metal ring, with eight to twelve strings attached, on which your staff can transport a tennis ball. The challenge in this version, is for several groups to simultaneously deposit their tennis balls onto a PVC "candelabra." After working independently in small groups, this activity will require your entire staff to come together.

You can make your own bull ring from a 1 1/2-inch (38 mm) diameter metal ring and ten strings each 10 feet (3 meters) long. The plastic cone or parking stand shown in the photograph is a large-volume sewing thread spool that has been recycled. You can also use an empty film canister or soda bottle as a parking place for the bull ring and tennis ball.

The PVC candelabra is made from a set of Teamplay Tubes (available from Training Wheels, Inc.) Using a variety of connectors and different lengths of half-inch PVC tubing, create a tower where several tennis balls can rest. You'll need to create a stable base for the tower and rest positions that are at different heights. It is a good idea to create one more rest location than the total number of tennis balls being transported.

Three bull ring groups is the perfect number for each candelabra. For every additional group added above this number (four or five, for example) you'll add another ten to fifteen minutes of maneuvering (and this can be frustrating for some groups). For groups of fifty or more staff members, consider using multiple PVC candelabras or try the large world-class bull ring shown in the photograph at the end of this activity.

In order to prepare your staff for the challenge of bringing three bull rings together in a very small space, we recommend that they practice the following sequence of basic skills. These three stages will teach the skills required to successfully complete this activity.

Stage One: Organize three groups of bull rings in a triangular pattern and invite your staff to join a group. Drop the bull ring over a suitable stand and stretch the strings outward like spokes of a wheel. Next, place a ball on top of the stand. Tennis balls are ideal for this activity, but other balls (golf balls, smile-faced balls, soft balls, etc.) are other possibilities. In stage one, the goal of the group is to lift the ball up into the air with the bull ring, and then lower it back down to the parking stand. Each person is requested to only hold the very end of the strings. If you have more strings than people, one person is allowed to hold two strings, but again, only at the very end. If one of your staff groups literally *drops the ball,* encourage them to assess what went wrong and try another technique until they are successful. This stage is designed to help your staff build skills lifting and lowering the tennis ball without dropping it.

Stage Two: Request each group to pick up the ball with the bull ring apparatus. Next, rotate their group 180 degrees (halfway) and place the ball back onto the parking stand. As an additional challenge, you can invite every person to close one eye while lowering the ball back to the parking stand. This reduction in depth perception will require more communication between the members of the group. This stage is designed to help your staff move as a unit with limited sight capabilities.

Stage Three: This final stage will take the three individual groups and encourage them to work together as one large group. Invite each of the three groups to lift their tennis ball with the bull ring and then to place it down on a different parking stand in the area. This generally requires all three groups to coordinate their efforts and move simultaneously to another position. Finally, request that all three groups lower their tennis balls so they touch down at exactly the same time. This final stage reinforces working as part of a larger group, coordinating with other groups, and timing the delivery of their tennis ball.

Once these warm-up stages have been successfully completed, your staff will be ready for the challenge of the Bull Ring Candelabra initiative.

BOX 3.9

I once was asked to work with a group of students from various county schools. Since several students were present from each of three different schools, I thought that the candelabra version of this activity would *bring them together*. With limited time, I explained the task and began the activity. It quickly became clear that without adequate practice and preparation (i.e., the three sequential stages described here) the chance for success in this activity was limited at best.

The very next time I used this activity, I was determined to set my teams up for success. By giving them the opportunity to fine tune their motor skills, to learn from their mistakes, and to sequentially begin the process of learning higher and higher level skills with the bull ring, they were indeed successful in placing all three balls on the candelabra. In fact, since that time, nearly every one of the groups that has participated in the three sequential stages has been successful in the final big-finish stage.

Jim Cain

A variation of the multiple group bull ring initiative that does not require the use of the PVC candelabra is to have three or more groups simultaneously touch their tennis balls together in mid-air. Like the candelabra version, this variation will bring your staff much closer together in order to accomplish the task.

For very large groups, here is a world-class version of the bull ring activity.

Courtesy of archiv faszinatour.de

A Creative Debriefing Technique

At the completion of this activity, your entire staff will be standing in a large circle. Take this opportunity to teach them the following debriefing or reviewing activity called Shuffle Left/Shuffle Right.

With your entire team standing in a complete circle, invite everyone to shuffle to the left. When someone in the group says, "Stop!" because they have a comment to share, the group stops and listens to this single individual. When they have finished their comment, they say, "Shuffle right" or "Shuffle left," and the group moves until another person says, "Stop!"

You can suggest the theme of the debriefing comment, such as, "Tell me what you think about how our group worked together in this activity."

This technique for review provides several valuable attributes. First, the person saying *stop* has the immediate and full attention of the rest of the group. For staff members with limited public-speaking experience, this respectful technique gives them uninterrupted attention of the entire group. Second, there is no discussion or rebuttal to anyone's comments. This allows everyone to have their say, without fear or concern. Next, for some groups, when they sit down they shut down. Shuffle Right/Shuffle Left keeps the group active, moving and energized. And finally, this activity is self-regulating for duration. Inform the group that any time the circle travels a complete 360-degree rotation, with no one saying, "Stop!" that this activity will conclude. Some staff members might need a significant portion of that rotation to form their comments, so be patient. Your staff will let you know when this review has come to its inevitable conclusion.

BOX 3.10

You can find more creative debriefing techniques (over one hundred, in fact) in the book *A Teachable Moment* by Jim Cain, Michelle Cummings and Jennifer Stanchfield, 2006, Kendall/Hunt Publishers, ISBN 0-7575-1782-X.

Notes

▬ 10. A Circle of Connection

After your team has progressed through the stages of group development outlined in Chapter 4, there will be a natural time for the following activity. Although most groups

utilize A Circle of Connection as a closing activity, you can also employ this activity as a way of demonstrating the connection that exists between the members of your staff at any time of your staff training program. Unity, community, and connection can be powerful and positive metaphors for your staff, and this activity illustrates all three.

Begin this activity, which requires no equipment at all, with your entire staff gathered in a small area. One person begins by introducing themselves and sharing something related to the theme you wish to introduce with this activity.

Staff training themes include: the most valuable information you've learned during this training, what skills you bring to the team, what challenge you are most looking forward to in your job, and how you plan to use the knowledge you've gained here.

The first person, as they are speaking, places both hands on their hips, forming the first link of chain. At any time during their commentary, if another staff member shares or connects with the comment being made, they can approach the person talking and link arms with them. Only the first person arriving is allowed to make a link.

This second person then introduces themselves and begins to share additional information about the theme being discussed, until a third person can link with them. This activity continues until everyone has linked together. The final link is for the last person to keep talking until the first person can link with them. The final configuration of the group will be a large circle, tightly linked together—another powerful metaphor for your staff to experience. At this point, there is an opportunity to say, ". . . and by the way. Those things that link us together bring us a bit closer together, as well!"

A special thanks to Dick Hammond for sharing this wonderful activity. Dick is co-author along with Chris Cavert of the book *The Empty Bag,* a great collection of teambuilding activities that require no props at all.

"Every time we encourage people to 'circle up,' move through a series of activities and initiative problems and gather in the debriefing circle to share thoughts and feelings, we are giving them an opportunity to understand the need, the value, and the joy of being fully human in connection with other people."
—Tom Smith

"The need to literally make a circle is essential. We cannot understand the circle if we are sitting in rows, being lectured at. Even when our minds have forgotten the power of the circle, our bodies remember . . .".
—Christina Baldwin

"Gathering in circles is an ancient practice being revived in our time."
—Parker J. Palmer

"I imagine good teaching as a circle of earnest people sitting down to ask each other meaningful questions. I don't see it as the handing down of answers."
—Alice Walker

"He drew a circle that shut me out—Heretic, rebel, a thing to flout. But Love and I had the wit to win: We drew a circle that took him in."
—Edwin Markham

Thirty More Staff Training Activities

4

In addition to our collection of the Ten Best Staff Training Activities in the previous chapter, this chapter contains 30 additional activities that explore an even wider variety of staff training and development topics.

11. Handshakes

There is no single, universal greeting that works with everyone on our planet. Luckily for much of the Western World, a handshake is most widely accepted as the preferred gesture of greeting. Here is an activity that explores a variety of handshakes and has the added benefit of encouraging face recognition between the members of your staff. For groups of 50 or more staff members, it can be difficult for the newest staff members to recall everyone they've talked to during the day. This playful icebreaker will help.

Author Jim Cain likes to tell the following story during this activity:

When I first began traveling to work with groups, I was invited to northern Canada. On my second day, a local from the area introduced himself and said, "So, where are your from?" "How do you know I'm not from right here?" I said, to which he replied, "I don't think so, Jim. You don't sound the way we do up here. But if you want to blend in with the locals, I'll show you how we shake hands up here in the north country." He then proceeded to show me the lumberjack handshake.

One partner extends their right fist, thumbs up. The second partner makes a similar right-handed fist, grabbing their partner's thumb, and placing their own thumb straight up. The first partner then adds their own left hand (in a similar fashion), followed by the second partners left hand. Next, these two partners saw back and forth, saying one name on the forward stroke and the other on the backstroke. Jim—Ted. Jim—Ted. Jim—Ted.

After shaking hands in this manner, turn to your partner and say, "I would never forget your face. I would always remember you in a crowd." Then hold up one, two, or three fingers. Go find a new partner with the same number of fingers showing.

After traveling in northern Canada, I then traveled out to Minneapolis, Minnesota. Now, Minnesota is the land of ten thousand lakes. And the people of that area are largely of Norwegian heritage. So it is a pretty likely bet that when you meet a Minnesotan, they'll be both a Norwegian and a fisherman. And what kind of fisherman? Walleye, of course! So when you want to blend in with the locals in Minneapolis, here is a two-part handshake that you can use.

First, face your partner and throw both hands up in the air and say, "Yahhh [your partner's first name]." Then reach out you hand (with your sleeves rolled up) and—bypassing your partner's hand—slap your hand against his forearm (like the sound of a walleye slapping the bottom of the boat when you've landed a big one). Oh, I almost forgot, Norwegian walleye fisherman are mostly left-handed, so be sure to try this particular handshake left-handed as well.

Now turn to this partner and say, "See ya later, alligator." Now go find a new partner that feels the same way about broccoli that you do.

After visiting the Great Plains, I next traveled back to my home state of Ohio. A very friendly state, right there in the heartland of the country. Ohio is so friendly, we even have our own state handshake.

Face your partner and together raise both hands above your head, fingers touching to make a large letter O, and say, "O." Then shake hands and say, "Hi." Finally, make another large letter O and again say, "O." That's the Ohio handshake. Do it again!

Now say to your partner, "Don't go away, I'll be right back." Next find someone with the same color (or the same number) of eyes you have.

And finally, the New York [or the name of your local town here] coffee-drinker's handshake. Face your partner and ask them about their favorite hot beverage in the morning. Place an imaginary cup of this hot beverage in your left hand. Be careful not to spill it. Raise your right hand to high-five your partner, miss, bend at the waist, lift the leg closest to your partner, and grasp their ankle with your hand and shake.

Now say to this partner, "Meet me right here in a minute."

Well, like all good education, if that was the lesson, here comes the test! Find your lumberjack partner and shake hands. (Some confusion occurs as everyone goes off to find their lumberjack partner. Plenty of sawing motion, and name shouting.)

Then say, "Now your Norwegian Walleye fisherman partner." (Shouts of *yahh* are heard, and the sound of slapping.)

Next, find your Buckeye partner. (Sounds of O – hi – o are heard.) *And finally, find your coffee-drinking partner.*

If you happen to use this handshake icebreaker at the beginning of a staff training week, don't be surprised if you see partner's shaking hands in the same style at other times of your program. The mental image of your partner's face, their name and the handshake are now triggers for each other. Remembering, "Hey, that was the guy I did the Ohio handshake with," will typically trigger their name as well.

For even more staff specific training, you can invent handshakes with sport themes (baseball pitchers, bowling), geographic themes (for your area of the country—like the Wisconsin dairyman's handshake), corporate and business themes (IT programmers), or even job-related themes (plumber).

12. Walk & Talk

Here is an interesting technique for beginning to build connections with the members of your staff. The kinesthetic nature of this activity will energize your staff while they begin forming connection with the other members of the team. This activity requires no equipment, but it is helpful to have sufficient space for the entire group to walk together without bumping into each other.

Begin by inviting everyone to partner with someone they do not know yet. Explain to them that they are to take a three-minute stroll together with this person and to find out three things about each other that they have in common. Encourage participants to go beyond convenient similarities such as being the same height or wearing similar shoes. For example, perhaps both partners like to read, but if they dig deeper, they may find out they like the same author or have read the same book recently. Perhaps they both like Italian food, but by digging deeper discover that they enjoy the same restaurant or the same Italian dessert. It is this style of similarity that is the goal of this activity.

When people discover that they have something in common with others, it creates a unique bond. The love of pets, books, old movies, sporting events, TV shows, music, and food are all subjects that can create a sense of connection between people that enjoy these things.

When your staff have completed their walk and returned to the training area, invite them to share their most unique commonality with everyone in the group.

BOX 4.1 When it comes to creating a connection with others, a face to face encounter can seem almost confrontational. Walking side by side creates an atmosphere of connection, without continuous eye contact. Movement also stimulates the participants, and brings energy to the conversation. By combining an ice-breaking activity with movement, participants not only make connections with their partners—they also arrive back at their starting location with high energy.

Notes

🔲 13. Wrapped Around My Finger (WAMF)

Here is one of the best icebreakers and get-acquainted activities ever created. This activity encourages a deeper level of information sharing and self-disclosure.

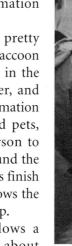

W.A.M.F. stands for Wrapped Around My Finger, and pretty much explains this entire activity. Begin with one unknotted raccoon circle for each group of four to six participants. One person in the group begins wrapping the webbing around an index finger, and while doing so, provides the group with some personal information (birthplace, family members, school experiences, childhood pets, dreams, goals, favorite foods, etc.). The goal is for this person to continue talking until the webbing is completely wrapped around the index finger. Given the length of the webbing, most participants finish in 60 to 120 seconds. When the person reaches the end, he allows the webbing to unwind and passes it to the next person in the group.

This particular technique allows a bit more time for folks to talk about themselves, and also provides a kinesthetic activity, coupled with a verbal activity for exploring some of the multiple-intelligence opportunities and whole-brain learning possibilities. There is also a popular theory that for folks who may be a bit shy about speaking to even a small group in public, the activity of wrapping the webbing around their finger occupies that portion of the brain that controls nervousness. By wrapping and rapping at the same time, the speech center becomes less inhibited, and more information is typically shared!

BOX 4.2 A Raccoon Circle is a 15 foot (4.6 meter) long segment of tubular climbing webbing. Raccoon circles come in many colors and can be used for more than 200 different icebreakers, team challenges, games, and other activities. You'll find more raccoon circle activities in this book, and you can download a small collection of raccoon circle activities at: www.teamworkandteamplay.com. Click on the "downloads" button in the main menu. If you'd like even more ideas for raccoon circles, *The Revised and Expanded Book of Raccoon Circles,* by Jim Cain and Tom Smith, is available from Kendall/Hunt Publishers (1-800-228-0810).

14. Autographs

Although you may have seen several versions of this classic get-acquainted activity, this particular version is unique. Instead of only one signature per block, this version of name bingo allows *anyone* to sign *any* block, making each person you meet the perfect person to autograph your sheet of paper. For example, one block asks the question, "Do you play a musical instrument?" If your answer is *yes,* you can sign your name in the upper blank portion of the box, and if your answer is *no,* you sign your name

in the lower portion of the box. Any one person can place their autograph in two different boxes on this page.

Begin this activity by inviting all participants to place their name in large letters in the upper-right corner of the sheet. This way, everyone they meet will have one more opportunity to learn their name. Instructions are also provided in the upper-left corner of each page, but don't be surprised if some participants still ask how to play this activity.

If you'd like to use this activity to teach your staff a valuable lesson, play for a few minutes, then stop and mention the following information compiled by Jim Cain during his extensive career working with corporations and professional groups:

BOX 4.3

In order for any organization to succeed, there are three critical ingredients they need. Think of these like the ingredients to the perfect apple pie recipe. If you have all three ingredients, in the correct amounts, your pie will taste wonderful. First, you need a **task** that is worth doing. For example, the organization Habitat for Humanity has a very worthy task, and there are many other organizations doing great work as well. But task alone is not enough. You need more ingredients to hold your organization together. Second, you need the chance for **growth** and to learn new things. The Public Broadcast System (PBS) has a theme of lifelong learning. A good organization needs this same ingredient. And finally, you need a chance to create and maintain positive **relationships** in the workplace. If your organization has all three of these critical ingredients, you'll have higher employee satisfaction, a greater retention of staff, and a much more pleasant work environment altogether.

Now in the activity you are now playing, what is the *task?* That's right, to fill my sheet with names. I want you to keep playing this same game, but I'd like to change the focus just a bit. As you continue, I want you to play in *relationship* mode. That is, if someone says they know someone famous, get their signature, but also ask them to tell you the story about meeting this person. If someone says they play a musical instrument, as them about it. In other words, get the signature, but also get the story that goes along with it.

Continue to play this activity, in relationship mode, for as long as the group's energy will allow. You'll find a full size version of this activity in the Ready-to-Copy section of this book.

Notes

The Big Question

If you could be the star of any Hollywood movie - what movie would you choose and what character would you play?

At the bottom of this paper write a question that you could ask to a fellow participant if you were to interview them for a local radio talk show. For example, you might ask questions such as:

1.   What was the most unusual job you have ever had?

2.   What is the definition of a life well lived?

3.   Who has been the most influential person in your life, and why?

You get the idea. Keep it clean, and be creative.

When you have finished writing your question, take this paper to the center of the room, find a partner, ask them your question, (they will answer it - you do not need to write the answer down) and then they will ask you their question (you answer it). When you are both finished talking, trade papers with this person. Then find a new partner - and ask them your new question.

Write your question here:

©Essential Staff Training Activities   Jim Cain, Clare-Marie Hannon & Dave Knobbe

15. The Big Question

This activity creates conversation between the members of your staff. It is also an ideal activity to begin a program when not everyone has yet arrived. You can start this activity with available personnel, and when more folks arrive, they can quickly create their own question and join the group.

Using the full-page document found in the Ready-to-Copy section of this book, each staff member writes a question. When meeting another member of the staff, they read the question on their sheet and their partner answers it. Their partner then reads the question on their sheet, and the first person answers it. When both partners have finished, they exchange papers and find a new partner and ask them their new question.

Here are a few interesting conversation starters that you can use for this activity:

- What movie have you seen more than once? Why?
- What can you do in your dreams that you cannot do in real life?
- What would you do if you knew that you could not fail?
- What is the best meal you have ever had in your whole life?
- Which teacher in your life was your favorite, and why?
- Name one thing you can do really well.
- What is the most interesting thing you have ever found?
- Tell me about your most interesting childhood friend.
- If you could have a million of anything (except money), what would you choose?
- What is the farthest you have ever been from home?
- What was the most helpful advice you were ever given?

16. The Big Answer

This activity is similar to the previous one, The Big Question, but in this case, every member of your staff can write a question for which they desperately want to know the answer. At the conclusion of your training program, this activity can help staff members ask a necessary question so that they completely grasp an important concept. Questions can also be aimed at upcoming events or projects for which all the details may not yet be available. Basically, this one activity allows staff members to openly and honestly admit that they need some assistance from the team to accomplish one of their goals. If even one of the answers is valuable, this entire activity will be viewed as outstanding. More often, several answers are useful, and lead to even more possibilities in the future.

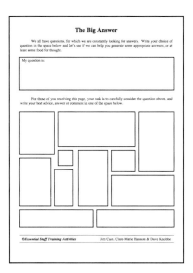

Using the full-page document found in the Ready-to-Copy section of this book, each staff member poses a question and writes it on the page provided. These pages are then circulated around the group, and everyone tries to provide their best written advice in answering each question. When each page eventually returns to its author, there will be several suggestions, comments, and bits of advice from fellow staff members for them to consider.

The significant problems we have cannot be solved at the same level of thinking with which we created them.
—Albert Einstein (1879–1955)

Each problem that I solved became a rule which served afterwards to solve other problems.
—Rene Descartes (1596–1650)

It is better to know some of the questions than all of the answers.
—James Thurber

---

17. Leadership Dance

Here is a wonderful energizer for any group. It also happens to be a very unique leadership activity. Begin by organizing your staff into groups of about eight participants. You'll need one piece of music for each person in a group. Each musical selection should be between 30 and 60 seconds long. You'll also need sufficient room for your entire staff to move about freely. Invite each group to count off from one to eight, and for each person to remember their number.

The opportunity in this activity is for each member of a group to lead their group when their selection of music is played. Participants do not know in advance what music style they will be asked to lead. This is truly a leadership challenge.

Here are a few tips to help you create the best collection of songs for your Leadership Dance. First, make sure to use music with a definite 'beat.' Marching band songs work great. You can also use a diverse collection of music that mimics the diversity of your staff. Many libraries have a music collection that explores various types and styles of music (from classic rock to country to hiphop to showtunes). You can even include television theme songs. If your staff training (or organization) has a theme, choose music that reinforces that theme. Be sure to limit the length of the song to no more than one minute in length. When you are leading a song that goes on and on, one minute can seem like a very long time!

Also, be sure that you have a music system that adequately amplifies the sound, so that all participants can hear the music and the rhythm.

BOX 4.5

As part of a week-long senior management retreat, the leadership dance provided two critical components. First, it was an excellent energizer for the 18 bank vice-presidents who had just consumed a very large lunch and were likely to nod off as a result. Second, it provided a unique opportunity for executives to demonstrate their ability to lead, even when they weren't exactly sure what was about to happen. Debriefing this activity included some discussion related to which leaders did the best job getting their group to follow them. Although some people are great dancers, they are not necessarily great leaders. What did the great leaders do that made it easy to follow them?

Notes

If you can walk you can dance, if you can talk you can sing.
—Zimbabwean Proverb

Dance like no one is watching—
Sing like no one is listening—
Love like you'll never be hurt—
Live like it's heaven on earth.
—Unknown

Dancing if madness to those that can't hear the music.
—George Carlin

18. Pieces of a Puzzle

Here is a challenging mystery that can be presented in 14 pieces, written on strips of paper. This can be a particularly enlightening activity when exploring differences in the personality and works styles of your entire staff. Myers-Briggs (MBTI), DiSC, True Colors, and other useful tools typically rank or organize participants into various

categories of behavior, style, or personality. You might be surprised to know that all groups can typically solve this puzzle, but often use different techniques. If you wish to use this type of activity with your staff, organize them into similar work styles and ask them to keep a record of their problem solving and solution techniques. The differences in their problem-solving techniques can lead to an interesting and informative reviewing session at the completion of this activity.

To perform Pieces of a Puzzle, copy or write the following information on separate pieces of paper and give one complete set to each group attempting to solve the puzzle. Divide the clues evenly between the members of the group. Each person may read the information on their paper strip out loud to the other members of the group, but no one else may look at their information. This is to encourage conversation and clear communication. The goal is for the group to discover and solve the puzzle. One of the clues (#4 to be specific) poses a question for the group to answer.

You'll find a complete copy of this challenge in the Ready-to-Copy section of this book. Simply make a photocopy of the page, cut out the clues, and you are ready to investigate how your staff members approach a problematic situation.

Pieces of a Puzzle for Staff Training

- Each staff visited the same four training locations, but in a different order.
- The first place the Australian group visited was Texas.
- Wyoming was the third training location the Australian group visited.
- In what order did the Italian group visit the training locations?
- The group that bought cell phones started their tour in Boston.
- Some information is irrelevant and will not help solve the problem.
- The English group visited Boston before Texas.
- The Italian group bought iPods in Wyoming.
- The Italian group visited New York after Boston.
- The Australian group received CPR training in Wyoming.
- Each staff visited their favorite training location last.

- Of the different staffs, the Dutch group liked Texas best.
- The Dutch group bought cell phones on their tour.
- The ACA took four staffs from four different countries on a tour of four training locations.

Solution techniques for many groups include some form of matrix analysis. Some liken this approach to a Sudoku puzzle. Although other team members cannot read your clues, it is OK for someone to write down all the information so that everyone can read it. Some groups find just the information requested and stop there. Some groups fill in the entire matrix so they know who went where when.

Although the only information requested is the order in which the Italian staff visited the four training locations, here is the complete listing for all groups.

TABLE 4.1

Answers to Pieces of a Puzzle for Staff Training

Dutch	English	Australians	Italians
Boston	New York	Texas	Wyoming
Wyoming	Boston	New York	Texas
New York	Texas	Wyoming	Boston
Texas	Wyoming	Boston	New York

Problems worthy of attack—prove their worth by fighting back.
—Piet Hein

▓ 19. Arrowheads

For all those times when your staff say that they don't have enough stuff to get the job done, here is the perfect activity. Arrowheads is a simple puzzle with a very significant teachable moment about the use of available resources.

The arrowhead puzzle shown here consists of seven pieces. You can make your own puzzles from the pattern provided in the Ready-to-Copy section of this book, or purchase them from Training Wheels, Inc. The challenge is to use these seven pieces to make a total of five arrowheads. There is one complete arrowhead in the collection, and it is one of the five arrowheads. All other arrowheads will be this same size and identical shape. When finished, your group will be able to see all five arrowheads at the same time.

Most groups struggle to create four different arrowheads and then typically comment to the facilitator, "There aren't enough pieces to make a fifth arrowhead." To which you can reply, "You have sufficient resources to complete the task." Of course, this requires some out-of-the-box thinking. You can further assist your team with clues such as, "It is important to get your arrowheads pointed in the same direction," or "In our organization, we like to march in a two-by-two formation."

The solution to this puzzle comes from using each available resource to create more than just one arrowhead. In this case, the four primary arrowheads can be assembled in a two-by-two pattern to frame a fifth arrowhead in the center. The contribution of each individual arrowhead is *more* than just one! This is a synergistic relationship.

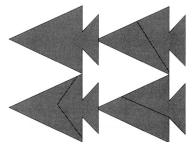

At this point you can debrief this activity or further explore synergy by asking the group, "If we combine four of these puzzles, how many arrowheads can we produce?" The answer—an amazing 25!

The teachable moment in this activity comes from realizing that even when there appears to be insufficient resources, if you use the resources you have creatively, you can often do more with less. Let's take this concept a step further, and graphically illustrate exactly what collaboration and synergy can mean to your organization.

Imagine that you have one employee creating the training manuals for your organization. With the recent hiring of more employees, you are going to need more manuals very soon, so you hire nine additional employees to perform this task. You're good at math, so you calculate that if one employee can produce ten training manuals in a week, ten employees should be able to produce 100 training manuals in that same week. Although the mathematics in this example are simple, the organizational culture is not. For some organizations, a tenfold increase in manpower will yield a tenfold increase in output. For synergistic organizations that are efficient, a tenfold increase in manpower can yield greater than a tenfold increase in output. Unfortunately, this same concept works in reverse. For organizations that are struggling, a tenfold increase in manpower not only does not produce a tenfold increase in output, but the overall efficiency of the entire organization goes down with change.

Graphically, this information looks like the illustration. The real goal, then, is to create the kind of environment where additional staff members not only cover their share of the work, but enhance the output of others in the organization. As a reviewing tool for the Arrowhead puzzle, make a list with your staff about which factors contribute to a positive culture and environment and which ones create a negative return on investment. This is the ideal place to discuss attitude, behavior, individual contributions and team performance. By identifying those factors that not only contribute to a positive atmosphere, but also those that diminish it, your team can create a strategy for keeping their work environment positive and rewarding. Keep this list in a public place in your organization. When someone demonstrates a behavior not in keeping with the group's ideals, reinforce the positive cultural values your group helped create.

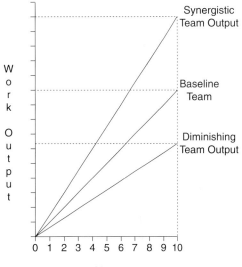

The Arrowhead Puzzle is a great activity to help your team understand the value of synergy. Synergy can be described metaphorically as: 1 + 1 = 3. Synergy exists when the output of a team is greater than the output of each individual combined. The illustration here demonstrates this point. If one team member can produce one unit of output and we hire nine additional team members, we expect to be able to produce a total output of ten units. If our team members work synergistically, they can actually produce more than ten units of output. Conversely, if our team members do not work synergistically or even worse, reduce each other's effectiveness, less than ten units of output will be produced. From this simple analysis you can see that teams operating synergistically have a substantial advantage over teams that do not.

BOX 4.6

There is a government building in Siena, Italy, the Palazzo Pubblico or town hall, which contains a visual version of the factor list mentioned here. *The Allegory and Effects of Good and Bad Government* frescoes by Ambrogio Lorenzetti is a series of several stunning portraits of the effects of good and bad governmental practices. It is rumored that town officials used this room during debates on critical issues. Whenever anyone made a suggestion that incorporated behaviors in the bad government illustrations, someone was sure to point to this image and say, "We don't want that kind of government." That makes this series of illustrations one of the first group contracts in history.

You can find images of these frescoes and information about Siena at

http://en.wikipedia.org/wiki/Palazzo_Pubblico
http://www.scholarsresource.com/browse/work/-1436218325

Notes

The greatest achievement of the human spirit is to live up to one's opportunities and make the most of one's resources.
—Vauvenargues

■ 20. Not Knots

Here is an activity to help your staff learn valuable consensus building skills. You'll need a 10 foot (3 meter) long segment of rope to create a rope *doodle*. The challenge of this

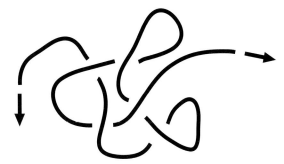

activity is for individual staff members to decide whether they think the rope will create a knot, or not, when the ends of the rope are pulled in different directions.

After creating the rope doodle invite your staff to view your creation: "In a minute, I am going to grasp each end of the rope and pull my hands apart. When I do, this rope might form some kind of knot. It might also form a straight line with no knot. Go with your gut instinct. If you think this mess will form a knot, stand over here on the knot side (right side). If you think this doodle will not make a knot, but rather a straight line, stand over here on the straight line side (left side)."

At this point, staff members are probably present on both sides. Consensus certainly does not exist at this moment. It can take significant time for a group in this situation to talk themselves into consensus, and let's face it, this isn't even a major life decision. Knot or not? So offer your staff a tool that they can use to help create consensus. Invite every person on the knot side to take a partner from the straight-line side. Both of their jobs are to argue passionately about their beliefs, and to try to convince the other person why they are correct. This process is called *pairing and sharing*. The catch is that at the end of two minutes *both partners must stay together*, and go to one side or the other. Consensus must be achieved.

Even after pairing and sharing, there is likely to be no clear decision on whether this rope doodle will produce a knot or a straight line. Rather than pulling the rope quickly, creating winners and losers, pull the rope *slowly* and allow individuals to change sides at any time they choose. This process has been referred to by John Maxwell as *failing forward*. The act of making a mistake can help us move forward in our search of better methods, techniques, and decisions. Use this technique, and at the end of this activity, you'll have all of your staff not only on the same side, but on the right side.

The exact formation of the rope doodle does not matter for the sake of this activity, but be sure to create this rope doodle before your staff are close enough to view it. Here is another example of a rope doodle.

---

21. The Change Train

Begin with 'trains' of four people, standing in a column. The first person is the engine; the last person is the caboose. Ask each of the cars behind the engine to place both hands on the shoulders of the person in front of them. If the conductor (the facilitator) yells, "Change!" the first person moves to the end of their own train, and becomes the caboose. If the conductor says, "Switch," the people in position two and three change places. If the conductor says, "Rotate," each person turns individually and faces the other way.

Now encourage the trains to begin moving, and keep moving even while attempting to follow the conductor's commands. Change. Switch. Rotate. Change-Rotate. Switch-Change-Switch.

Chances are that no groups of four in this activity have performed flawlessly to this point. Here is where the opportunity exists to help your staff move beyond a simple and playful activity and explore a valuable job-related skill. Invite each train of four people to practice on their own for a few minutes. Work through each of the commands. Help each other be successful.

After your staff have had the chance to help each other improve, you can increase the challenge level of this activity. Inform each train that they have entered a tunnel where it is completely dark. *"Close your eyes, but try to still follow my commands. Help each other."* Change. Switch-Rotate. Change-Rotate-Switch-Change.

As a debriefing discussion, ask each group what they would need to do so that they could perform any of these commands flawlessly. It is also a great idea to ask participants what happened in their group when someone made a mistake. Did the other members of the group perhaps give them a push in the right direction? A helpful push in the right direction from a colleague is a great opportunity to discuss mentoring and coaching in the workplace.

22. Peteca

A Peteca is a hand version of hackysack, similar to the shuttlecock used in badminton, but hit with the hands instead of a racket or paddle. The origin of this activity is primarily from Brazil, but versions of this game are played in many countries around the world. Some organizations have proposed making Peteca one of the sports played at the Olympic games.

The Peteca can be used during your staff trainings for several useful purposes. First, the physical and kinesthetic movement associated with playing this game has an energizing effect without requiring strenuous effort. Second, there are sufficient variations for this activity, so you can introduce it more than once, with new rules and requirements, and encourage your staff to adapt to change and modifications in their work environment. Finally, after experiencing a variety of playing methods, your staff will be prepared to discuss how to include creative twists and ideas in their own work environment. They can take the common and sometimes repetitive tasks they regularly perform and adapt them to make them more fun. Just consider the work environment of the Seattle fish market. The workers at Pike Place Fish modified their regular duties to become one of the classic case studies in boosting employee morale and improving results. The book *FISH!* by Stephen Lundin, Harry Paul, and John Christensen, explores this phenomenon.

The Peteca doesn't require much in the way of audience preparation to be successful. With circles of eight to twelve people, give the following instructions. "Everyone, hold your hands open in the palms up position. Your job is to keep this Peteca in the air for a total of at least 21 hits, using just your hands. Ready? Go!"

In the first round, your staff members will be building skills playing a game that is probably brand new to them. You will probably see the Peteca fall to the ground several times during this round. After a few minutes, encourage your staff to discuss what is working and what is not in their group. These kinds of discussion during play take this activity from a simple game to a teaching tool for your staff. After the "what works/what doesn't" conversation, invite your staff to try again, but this time using only their nondominant hand.

Your staff's proficiency with this activity will increase with practice. Here is a complete list of the variations we like to use with the Peteca. The goal in each round is to achieve at least 21 hits without dropping the Peteca.

1. Hit the Peteca using either hand.
2. Hit the Peteca using only the nondominant hand.
3. Using either hand, but standing (balancing) only on one foot.

4. Using either hand, stand on two feet, but clap three times after each hit before being allowed to hit the Peteca again.

5. After hitting the Peteca, participants must spin 360 degrees before hitting it again.

6. After hitting the Peteca, participants must high-five someone before hitting it again.

7. A whole brain learning variation in two parts: In part one, participants say their own name when they hit the Peteca. In part two, participants must say the name of another member of their group when hitting the Peteca, and nobody can say the same name twice in a row! This version requires both sides of the brain—a kinesthetic activity for one side, and a memory word recall for the other.

8. As a final bonus round, challenge each group to play their favorite variation and attempt to reach the highest number of hits that they can.

BOX 4.7

You can download an extensive file about Petecas, which are also called indiacas, funderbirds, and featherballs in other parts of the world, at www.teamworkandteamplay.com/resources.html. Click on The Featherball document for more than 20 pages of useful information about this unique activity. You'll find instructions for making your own Peteca, international rules for competitive play, and more ideas for making the Peteca a useful part of your next staff training program. You can also purchase Petecas from Training Wheels, Inc.

Notes

▪ 23. Pop It

With this activity, a few dozen balloons, and a single thumbtack or push-pin, you can explore workplace expectations and responsibilities with your staff.

No matter how much training we provide staff, it is likely that the first week on the job will be an even more powerful learning experience. If supervisors aren't available to coach and provide positive feedback during the first few days of a new job, new staff members are likely to look to other staff members to determine what it takes to be successful, which rules are "real," and which procedures can be ignored. On the back page of this book is a fairly profound statement, *"If you're not going to talk to your staff about character—who is?"* But even more profound is the statement, *"If you're not going to teach your new employee the best of the culture in your organization—who is?"* Your staff are going to learn the culture of your organization from somebody. Who do you want to teach them?

One of the most profound insights from this activity is for supervisors to realize the value in being visible and providing advice, direction, and positive feedback to new employees. Showing these employees a clear vision of what a successful staff member contributes is very important. It is also helpful to see that new staff members determine what is important in a work setting by watching how supervisors respond to the behaviors, attitudes, and actions of other staff members. They quickly determine which rules and procedures are necessary and which ones can be avoided or disregarded.

Pop It creates an experience of nonspecific job responsibilities, unknown expectations, and very immediate and often critical (but nonspecific) feedback. In short, this activity explores the worst of performance appraisals and supervisory feedback, and in doing so, creates the opportunity to discuss ways to greatly improve this process.

You'll need three to four dozen balloons (any shape, and with a variety of colors) for this activity. Begin by joining your staff in a circle, seated in chairs. As the quality control monitor for this balloon production facility, you have complete authority for declaring a balloon acceptable or a reject. Instruct your staff to blow up all the balloons, tie them with a knot, and pass them to you, one at a time for inspection. For balloons that meet your exacting (but as yet, unidentified) standards, simply say, "Acceptable," and toss them back to the center of the circle. Your response to unacceptable balloons is a bit more dramatic. When you are passed an unacceptable or reject balloon, take the push-pin or thumbtack and immediately *pop it.*

The challenge for your staff is to discover the criteria for what makes an acceptable balloon and what makes a reject balloon.

During this process, your staff will often try various techniques and await your response to their contributions. This is not unlike some work environments. Ultimately, the goal here will be to engage our staff in understanding their roles, responsibilities, and expectations completely, so that when they finish a task, they won't wonder whether it is acceptable or not. They'll know for sure!

You can choose any two criteria for designating an acceptable balloon, based on the size, direction of delivery, color, shape, and order they arrive at your quality inspection station. Our favorite combination of criteria is this:

Staff members must pass a balloon to you using their left hand only. Anyone passing you a balloon with their right hand has created an unacceptable balloon—Pop It!

If two balloons of the same color are passed, even correctly, the second one is considered a reject.

As a reviewing technique, explain to the participants that the balloons represent all the things that staff members might choose to do in the work setting. Ask them to identify what some of those behaviors are (be sure to elicit both acceptable and unacceptable choices).

"Staff members make choices in the workplace to meet their needs and to be successful. Some choices lead to successful completion of tasks and others do not. When staff are new to an assignment, they may not be completely sure of what criteria a supervisor will use to assess their performance. When that happens, they may start trying all kinds of things (experimenting) to see what they need to do and sometimes, what they can get away with. Let's see how this plays out with these balloons."

"For today's task, your staff team's job responsibility is to acceptable balloons. Since this is a simple part of the job and you have received extensive training on our mission and goals as well as processes, it is assumed you can carry out this task successfully. When you deliver acceptable products, the quality control inspector will tell you, but unacceptable balloons will be rejected and popped. Your job is to figure out the criteria for acceptable and unacceptable balloons in this work environment. Ready, begin!"

At this point, your staff will begin delivering balloons to you for inspection. Typically, they try a variety of techniques and strategies to collect some data. If a balloon is accepted, they will try to understand why. Sometimes their reasoning is correct, other times it may not be. Some workers may get frustrated if several of their products are labeled rejects. The behavior, attitude, and actions of the group in this environment will create valuable discussion topics during the final debrief of this activity. If your staff run out of balloons before identifying the factors that create an acceptable or unacceptable balloon, instruct them to blow up more balloons. After all, *they can't expect supervisors to do their work for them!*

Eventually, most groups begin to see patterns in their delivery system, and identify one or both of the acceptability criteria. Encourage your staff to test their hypothesis with additional balloons. As they begin to deliver acceptable balloons consistently, praise their efforts.

When the group has presented their criteria for creating and delivering acceptable balloons, ask some of the following questions, but first share the exact criteria:

- How similar were the staff's assumptions to the actual acceptability criteria?
- Which was more obvious, success or failure?
- What did it take to figure out how to be a successful contributor?
- How did it feel for you when you couldn't get the quality control inspector (your supervisor) to be clear about the criteria for acceptability? How did it impact your relationship with your supervisor when they kept popping your balloons?
- Where did you look for information about being successful when it wasn't clear from your supervisor?
- How did your group start to collaborate to figure out what they needed to do? Did it help or hurt the process?
- What did staff need from their supervisor to avoid the frustration and wasted energy that this process consumed?
- How can you work with your supervisor to ensure that you know what it takes to be successful?

BOX 4.8

Many of the staff supervisors I work with also have program development and management responsibilities. When pressed, many will admit that they were attracted to the job by the program side and that supervision is their *least favorite part of the job*. Convincing young managers to spend significant time, in the first few weeks on the job observing, providing feedback, and coaching for success is always challenging. This can be further complicated by staff members who want coaching and support but are nervous about being criticized by their supervisor. When I have the opportunity to work with supervisors before training the entire staff, I use this activity as a lead-in to a discussion about how they are going to allocate enough time to be sure staff feel like their performance matters and know how to be competent at their job. We repeat the activity with the entire staff as a means to opening a dialogue between staff members and supervisors about expectations and opportunities for performance feedback.

Clare-Marie Hannon

⬛ 24. Inside/Out

Here is a great example of how a simple Raccoon Circle activity can be used to instruct more than just one staff-training topic. Traditionally Inside/Out has been used to explore ethical behavior in the workplace, as shown in the first summary. Ethical behavior is no doubt a worthy and important topic for a staff training session, but author Clare-Marie Hannon has taken this activity even farther by incorporating the valuable skills of learning how to solve problems collectively as a team. This topic is covered in the second part of this activity description.

Inside/Out—A Lesson in Ethical Behavior

Here is a Raccoon Circle activity that explores ethical behavior in the workplace. There aren't many engaging activities that can meet this unique need, but Inside/Out does the job very nicely.

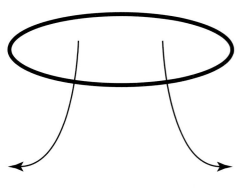

Begin with a Raccoon Circle on the floor. Have a group of five to seven participants step inside the circle. The task is now for the entire group to go from the inside of the circle to the outside, by going underneath the Raccoon Circle, without anyone in the group using their hands, arms or shoulders.

In order for each member of the group to assist in the completion of the task, they need to know the plan and what their part is in the solution. To this end, encourage the group to "plan their work" and then "work their plan." This means that prior to ANY action, the group will need to plan their approach to solving this problem, and making sure that everyone in the group knows their part of the plan. Encourage an 'off site' planning meeting, where participants move away from their Raccoon Circle to plan their work, and then return to work their plan.

Once all groups have completed Inside/Out, invite them to perform the same challenge in reverse, Outside/In, going from the outside of the circle to the inside, again without using their arms or shoulders or hands.

After completing the task, most group members will feel that they followed the rules and successfully completed the task. As a check, ask if anyone in the group crawled on their hands and knees to exit the circle. Or used their hands to hold up a leg, or balance against another person. The rules stated, "without using your arms or shoulders or hands," but most people interpret this to mean that you cannot touch the Raccoon Circle with your arms or shoulders or hands. In this case, this ambiguity in interpretation is the invitation to discuss what ethical behavior means in the workplace. *"How many people saw another person using their arms or shoulders or hands? How many said something about this? How can be expect our staff to follow the rules if we don't?"*

As a further step, ask the group how you as an instructor could have been more clear in presenting the rules. It appeared that you were, by saying, *"without using your arms or shoulders or hands,"* but the behavior of the group didn't support this assumption. What would have made your instructions more clear?

Inside/Out—Learning to Solve Problems as a Team

Although many individuals possess skills in problem solving, it can be a significant challenge to perform this task as part of a team or within a group setting. The activity Inside/Out will be used to help your staff develop a common language and useful skills related to a team problem-solving process.

Problem Solving in Nine Steps

The ability to solve challenges in a team setting is a valuable skill in many organizations. Although this ability requires a variety of actions, the following nine-step process should clarify the most critical components in the problem-solving process.

1. **Define the problem.** Be sure everyone in the group clearly understands the problem, its parameters (rules), and its goals.
2. **Decide if the problem is important.** Decide as a group if the problem is important enough to solve and if the group has enough energy and resources to solve the problem.
3. **Gather information.** Collect data and information through direct observation, questioning, and physical contact with the resources.
4. **Generate ideas.** Begin to create ideas that could potentially solve the problem. Avoid quick judgment and encourage combining ideas.
5. **Develop a plan.** The group identifies which ideas they want to try first. Some ideas may be eliminated. Multiple ideas can appear in the final plan. Task assignments and priorities are also part of the plan.
6. **Communicate the plan and gain consensus.** Be sure that everyone in the group fully understands the plan and agrees to give their best effort to help the plan succeed.
7. **Try the plan.** Carry out the plan to solve the problem. The plan may have to be modified as the group progresses, requiring a return to an earlier step.
8. **Evaluate the outcome.** Once the group carries out the plan, they must decide if they have solved the problem by measuring the outcome.
9. **Celebrate success or return to the first step to try again.** If the group concludes that they have solved the problem, it is time to celebrate! Acknowledge the contributions within the group that made it possible to solve the problem. If the group determines that they have not solved the problem, they return to earlier steps and continue working through this process.

Introducing the Problem-Solving Process with Inside/Out

You'll need one Raccoon Circle per group of nine participants, one set of nine problem-solving cards (available in the Ready-to-Copy section of this book), one

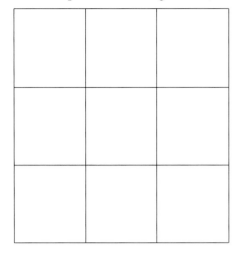

very large illustration of the nine-block problem-solving "window" created on a shower curtain (with each of the nine blocks at least 2 feet [60 cm] square), a smaller table-size version of the nine-block window drawn on a flip-chart page with colorful markers, and one soft throwable object (such as a stuffed animal or beanbag) for this introduction to the problem-solving process.

Prepare for this activity by placing the large window model on the ground. In the near future, participants will use this version of the problem-solving window to physically stand in the problem-solving stage they are exploring. As an alternative, participants can also throw the beanbag into the appropriate block to indicate their current focus.

Next, introduce the activity Inside/Out to each group while they are standing inside a knotted Raccoon Circle. *"Your challenge will be to move your group from inside the circle to the outside by passing under the circle. You must accomplish this without using your arms or shoulders or hands."* Encourage each group to move away from the Raccoon Circle for several minutes, to create a plan.

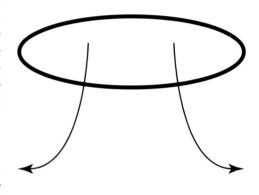

When all groups have their plan completed, invite them to return to the Raccoon Circle and perform this activity. If you have multiple groups performing this activity, some will generally complete the task before others. Invite those groups that finish quickly to repeat the process in the reverse direction (outside/in) with the same requirements.

When all groups have completed the task, produce the flip-chart-sized window illustration and ask each group to identify the various steps they took to accomplish this task. Write their contributions in the appropriate block of the window diagram. Be prepared to create a basic illustration of each of the nine steps previously identified in this book.

When asked, "What did you do to solve this problem?" groups often begin by discussing the *doing* part of the process. Hand them the "Do It" card and fill in this block of the window diagram. Ask your staff what they did before that step. Allow them time to think and prompt them until they have identified as many of the steps in the

above model as possible. Continue to fill in the window diagram and select one person from each group to receive the corresponding problem-solving card.

After each of the nine problem-solving steps have been identified by the group, ask them to evaluate how they did on each of these steps. *Did they complete each step? Did they spend too much or too little time in any step? Were they successful in solving the problem?* Many groups initially say yes, but then realize that they may have used their hands in a manner that violated some of the basic rules of the activity.

Remembering all nine steps of the problem-solving window model will no doubt require some additional work on the part of your staff. Here are some ideas for creating those opportunities. Notice that each technique sequentially increases their ability to familiarize themselves with and master this concept:

1. Using the flip chart illustration, allow staff to have read all nine steps aloud.
2. Using the problem-solving cards they possess, ask your group to stand in the correct order and identify each of their steps.
3. Using the large (and currently blank) illustration, stand in each box and ask your staff to name this step.

4. Turn the flip chart over (face down) and ask your staff to name the nine steps without seeing the window illustration.
5. With the group standing in a circle, toss a ball or other soft throwable object from person to person. The first person names the first step of the problem-solving process. The second person names the second step, and so on. If anyone needs prompting, encourage the rest of the group to provide assistance.

BOX 4.9

If your staff will be performing tasks with a strong team problem-solving component, it can be valuable to review the nine-step problem-solving model with them. Periodically revisit this model and review your staff's progress in effectively completing each step. Identify those steps that consistently challenge your staff and focus your future training opportunities on the skills required in these areas.

Different members of your staff are likely to have skills for different steps in the problem-solving process. A personality or work-style inventory (such as DiSC, MBTI, or True Colors) can provide added insight to help these team members identify their strengths and challenges in the problem-solving process. Identifying personnel with skills in specific steps of the problem-solving process recognizes their value to the team.

Notes

25. Tie the Knot

Teamwork is not necessarily easier. It is better, but it is not easier.
—Jim Cain

This activity is a great follow-up to the previous activity in this book, Inside/Out. It is ideal for practicing problem solving in small groups, and it presents a teachable moment by comparing the amount of time required for both an individual and a team to successfully complete a similar task. This activity explores a potential barrier to teamwork in small groups—the perception that it can be more efficient to contribute individually rather than to collaborate as part of a larger team.

Begin by distributing 7 feet (2.2 meters) of rope to every person in the group. Demonstrate tying an overhand knot in the middle of the rope, and instruct each person to create a similar knot in their rope.

"Tying a knot by ourselves is a pretty easy task, isn't it? There are times, however, when you'll need to include other staff members in a project, and this can lead to additional complications and require some necessary additional skills. Tools like the problem-solving process become more important when we have a complicated task that includes other people."

Next, ask your staff to form groups with four members, standing in a straight line. Place one rope between each person. You'll have one extra rope per team, which you can set aside for a few minutes. The group task is now to tie a knot in the middle of each rope. *"You've already proved that you can do this task by yourself. Now the challenge is to be able to do it as part of a team."*

Explain to your staff that this is an opportunity to use the problem-solving process. Provide a set of problem-solving cards (available in the Ready-to-Copy section of this book) to each group. Encourage them to refer to the various steps in this technique as they progress through their task.

Some groups are likely to finish before others. Invite them to visit other groups and coach them through the process. Remind them that coaches do not take over the leadership of the group, but, rather, provide encouragement, assistance, and support.

Coaches can also display the appropriate problem-solving cards for each stage of task completion that the group currently occupies.

When all groups have successfully completed the challenge, ask each group to discuss the following questions. You can provide these individually to each group on a piece of paper, or present one flip-chart page with all questions for the groups to discuss simultaneously.

- How did you define the problem?
- How did you decide it was important and possible?
- What kind of information did you gather?
- What kind of ideas did people in your group have?
- How did you develop your plan?
- What evidence was there that people had a good understanding of the plan and committed to it?
- How did the execution work for you?
- Were you successful?
- Did you celebrate?
- If you restarted, what step did you go back to?
- Why is this task so easy by yourself and so hard when you engage others?
- What do you have to do differently in order to engage others in solving the problem? When is it worth the effort to engage others in the projects and processes you are working on?
- What was most challenging about this activity?
- How can we as a staff avoid some of these challenges as we work together in the future?

Give groups ten to twenty minutes to discuss these questions and then ask each group to share their most interesting revelations about this activity.

It's so much easier to suggest solutions when you don't know too much about the problem.
—Malcolm Forbes (1919–1990)

BOX 4.10

One of the interesting dynamics in the Tie the Knot activity is that it is significantly easier to figure out how to tie knots in the two outside ropes (between participants 1 and 2 and participants 3 and 4) than it is to tie a knot in the middle rope (between participants 2 and 3). The people at the ends can tie the knot in these ropes with relatively little help from the rest of the group, and so they may assume that the people with the middle rope should be able to do the same thing. As a result, it is easy for them to step back and wait, rather than actively help to find a solution. In the end, the knot in the middle can only be tied if everyone is engaged and recognizes their connection to the process. This is a powerful demonstration of the old saying, "If you are not part of the solution you are part of the problem!"

I recently facilitated an organizational development retreat with a youth development agency that had the goals of moving from multiple programs on multiple sites to a more comprehensive set of services. Individuals who had previously operated separately managed programs were being asked to change their view of their contribution from *my program* to *our program*. It was easy for individuals to feel disengaged when the conversation turned to age groups and facilities that had traditionally been managed by someone else on the team. It took this activity to draw attention to the fact that the new organizational model required each director to view *all* programs and *all* sites as part of the programs they would manage in the future. By the time the retreat concluded, portions of the teen program had been moved to a site traditionally dedicated to younger participants and a plan was in place to involve these teens in serving as mentors for the younger participants. One staff member made the comment as the plan unfolded, "I'm so glad I got the push to realize my role in 'tying' all of this together!"

Clare-Marie Hannon

Notes

26. Finding Your People

Knowing and understanding where you belong in an organization is important for most employees. In the next ten years, most organizations are likely to become more culturally diverse than they are right now. Finding Your People is not only about knowing where you belong, but also about inviting others to join you. This activity

will help each of your staff members go beyond organizational and cultural boundaries and see everyone as part of *their people.*

You'll need a collection of three-dimensional wooden shapes for this activity. These can be obtained from craft or hobby stores or purchased from Training Wheels, Inc. The collection shown here contains a variety of colors and shapes, plus one unique star. If you make your own set for your staff, you'll need about five similar pieces in several different shapes, and a single one-of-a-kind shape. It makes the challenge a bit more interesting if some of your shapes are similar to each other.

Begin this activity by placing sufficient wood shapes (including the unique star) into a bag. Invite each member of your staff to take one piece from the bag, but not to look at it. This activity is a tactile and verbal one, not a visual one. Once every member of your staff has a wooden shape, the challenge is to find the other people in the group that have a similar piece. Participants are allowed to touch and describe their shape, but not to look at it. No one is allowed to touch or look at the shapes held by another person.

After several minutes of everyone *finding their people,* ask the group to stop and lock their feet in place. *"Now, without moving your feet, look at your shape."* At this point you'll hear your staff's surprise as they can easily tell what each shape is, compared to their often clumsy interpretation when they were without visual clues. Next, ask your staff where each of the shapes are. *"Where are the houses? Where are the trees? Where are the arrowheads?"* Finally, ask your staff, *"Where is the star?"* At this point, the one unique person in the group is identified. Ask this person what response they received from other members of the group when they were trying to *find their people.*

Now it is time to take this activity to a higher level. Ask everyone with a green piece of wood to hold it up. *"Look around. Aren't these some of your people? If you have a red shape, hold it up. Look around. These are some of your people, too. What do all of these shapes have in common?"* They are made of wood. *"What do all of us have in common? If we can answer that as a group, then everyone here will be one of your people!"* At this point, you'll have the complete attention of your staff. This is a great opportunity to talk about inclusiveness, community, and unity.

BOX 4.11

While I have enjoyed sharing this activity for a number of years now, it wasn't until recently that a friend suggested that I add a specific story to the end of the activity. Robert Fulghum, in his book *All I Really Need to Know I Learned in Kindergarten,* tells a wonderful story simply titled "The Mermaid." It is a great story that tells about fitting into the available boxes in our society. I recommend that you share this activity and this story with your staff. You can find this essay in the 15th anniversary edition of *All I Really Need to Know I Learned in Kindergarten* by Robert Fulghum, 2003, Ballantine Books, New York, ISBN 0-345-46617-9.

Notes

27. Magic Carpet

This is another excellent example of how a simple activity can create a teachable moment for your staff. In this collection of Magic Carpet activities, your staff members will be encouraged to set goals, discuss barriers to reaching these goals, creatively solve a problem, work together as a team, and celebrate together, too.

Let's begin with the basic magic carpet challenge. You'll need enough magic carpets for your entire staff. These can be created from plastic tarps, blankets, tablecloths or even shower curtains. You'll want to place eight to ten staff members on each magic carpet, with minimal space left over. Place other magic carpets nearby. The challenge is for the group to turn their magic carpet over without lifting anyone up, or touching the floor in the area surrounding each magic carpet.

BOX 4.12

I like to conduct activity #48 in this book, Grand Prix Racing, prior to the magic carpet initiative. The competitive nature of Grand Prix Racing places most participants in a noncollaborative frame of mind. After completing several rounds of racing, I ask each team to stand completely on their magic carpet. Next I instruct them to turn over their carpets without lifting anyone up and without touching the ground. I finish by saying six words that almost guarantee that these groups will compete rather than collaborate, *"Let's see which team finishes first!"*

Groups typically struggle at this point to perform the task by themselves. This is an opportunity to stop an activity in the middle, and create a discussion with the group. Many groups will respond, when asked what the two rules are, "without lifting anyone up and without stepping off the magic carpet." *"But I didn't say you couldn't step off. All I said was that you couldn't touch the ground. When in this activity did you become several separate teams instead of one single team?"* Most groups will reflect on the competitive nature of the previous activity, and realize that they reacted to a prior situation, instead of constantly working toward building a team. At this point,

ask each magic carpet team to begin again, and this time, look around for additional resources that can help you accomplish this task successfully.

Jim Cain

Magic Carpet with Goal Setting

Here is a technique for using the Magic Carpet initiative to include a goal-setting opportunity for each member of your staff. Place several magic carpets in close proximity to each other, and ask eight to ten staff members to stand around the perimeter of each carpet. Provide a piece of masking tape to each person and several ink (*not* felt marker) pens. Invite each person to write a job-related goal they have on this piece of masking tape, and firmly attach it to the top surface of the magic carpet. When all team members have completed this assignment, encourage them each to voice their goal to the other members in their group.

Next, turn over each magic carpet, and again provide participants with masking tape and pens. Invite your staff to write down any barriers they might see to reaching their goals. These can include budgetary limitations, time restrictions, resource issues, and other significant and real obstacles to the successful attainment of their original goal. Encourage all participants to share their list of barriers.

Now ask that everyone steps onto their magic carpet (which is now showing the barrier side). The challenge is for this group as a whole to reach their goals which are on the other side of each magic carpet, without lifting anyone up and without touching the ground in the space near each carpet.

Just as in the first example of the Magic Carpet initiative, most groups will attempt to turn over their carpets individually. Although a few groups may actually succeed with this technique, there is a better approach. Creatively using available resources (and looking for a win–win solution), several groups will no doubt help each other reach their goals.

At the completion of this activity, have two flip-chart pages ready with the words *goals* on one page and *barriers* on the other. Invite participants to place their goal and barrier tape on these pages. Keep these signs in the training area for future reference and discussion opportunities.

Additional review and debriefing topics can include the fact that many staff members might feel that they alone are responsible for reaching their goals, and that this task must be done entirely by themselves. The Magic Carpet initiative demonstrates that work groups are most effective when teams cooperate, collaborate, and help each other achieve success. The T.E.A.M. acronym, Together Everyone Achieves More (or in Spanish *Juntos Todos Tienen Mayores Logros*), is especially appropriate here.

Recent research on the millennial generation indicates that our youngest staff members have high expectations about the responsibility of management to be sure that they learn and grow in their job. In general, all of our staff are going to be more motivated if they are working toward something they understand and think is important. Staff members need to have the opportunity to identify what they want to achieve through their role as a part of the staff team. The chances of staff reaching their goals is increased when they share their goals with other members of the team and seek out support from the other people they will be working with. The goal-setting version of Magic Carpet gives each staff member the opportunity to identify and share goals and seek support from the team in overcoming barriers to reaching these goals. This is also a great opportunity for supervisors to begin a conversation with staff members about what will make their work experience valuable to them and to reinforce your organizational commitment to helping staff reach their goals.

I know of at least one summer camp director who keeps the list of masking tape goals for each of his staff members on the door to his office. Throughout the summer, he rereads this list and looks for opportunities to help his staff reach their goals. He also uses the list of barriers in meetings with his camp board, to help them create solutions to the obstacles identified by the camp staff.

Jim Cain

I once used the Magic Carpet activity while working with sixty day-care instructors as part of an in-service day of training. This is a group that often feels under-appreciated and underresourced. As one might expect, they were excited to have the opportunity to share their goals, both personal and professional. But the break-though for this group came when each group struggled for a considerable time to turn over their individual magic carpets. Comments like, "This is impossible, there just isn't enough space," filled the room. Finally, one group hesitantly asked if they could move a few people onto a nearby carpet. "Not our whole group—just a few people." When other groups in the room saw them they asked incredulously, *"Can you do that?"*

In the discussion that followed, teachers shared how isolated they felt in their classroom and how locked in they had become to seeing their resources as limited to that classroom alone. Individual instructors from this group committed to sharing resources not only within their facility but also to share resources with the other facilities in the area. Participants left that day with the support of a much larger network and a new system to help them reach their individual goals.

Clare-Marie Hannon

28. The Helium Stick

When teams of people first begin working together, it can be challenging to coordinate their efforts. The next chapter of this book discusses techniques for exploring the stages of group formation using active learning, including the critical *storming* stage. Suffice it to say that until the group can work through the coordination of their efforts, the best efforts of some individuals can actually sabotage the outcome of the group. How the group deals with this outcome ultimately determines the success or failure of the entire team. In the case of the appropriately named Helium Stick activity, the real goal is to get your staff's energy moving in the right direction!

For this activity, you'll need a lightweight but stiff pole or tube (such as a multisegment aluminum tent pole or small-diameter PVC tube). You'll need a pole that is about 12 inches (30 cm) long per person. A group of ten participants will require a pole that is ten feet (3 meters) long. This activity works best for groups of eight to fourteen participants per pole.

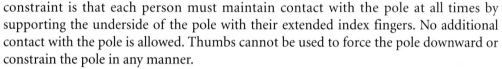

Divide the group into two halves and form lines facing each other. Ask the group to point in the direction that is commonly referred to as *up*. Next, ask them to point in the direction known as *down*. Just to reinforce this information, repeat pointing up and down again. Next, invite participants to place their hands like six-shooter pistols toward their partner. All hands in the group should be at the same uniform height.

Explain to the group that you have a simple challenge for them. In a moment you will place a pole on their extended index fingers. Their job is to lower the pole to the ground. The only constraint is that each person must maintain contact with the pole at all times by supporting the underside of the pole with their extended index fingers. No additional contact with the pole is allowed. Thumbs cannot be used to force the pole downward or constrain the pole in any manner.

When your group indicates that they understand the challenge, stand in the middle of the one side of the group, and horizontally lower a pole to slightly below the shoulder level of most participants. Allow each person to make light contact with the pole. On the count of three, let go of the pole.

Surprisingly, the tendency of the pole is to go *up*, rather than *down!* At this point, quickly grab the pole, and acting embarrassed, apologize to the group and say, *"My mistake. I must have done a poor job explaining the task. The goal was to lower this pole to the ground, not raise it. Let's try again, but first let's be sure we know which way is up from down. Could you all indicate the direction we refer to as up? And could you again show me which way is down? Everyone understand? OK, let's try again."*

Again, place the pole onto the hands of the group, holding the middle with a slight downward pressure until everyone in the group has light contact with the pole. On the count of three, let go.

The magic of the Helium Stick is caused by an imbalance in force. The tiny force of each finger in contact with the pole, when multiplied by the total number of fingers touching the pole, is greater than the actual weight of the pole. From a physics point of view, there is more force acting upward than gravity acting downward.

There is a process known as *sense-making* where individuals attempt to grasp the basis for things they at first cannot understand. Initial attempts at sense-making can be wildly imaginative, creative, and occasionally completely off target. It is this attempt at sense-making that produces such remarks as, "It must be magnetic," or "OK, who did that?" These remarks are the beginning of the group's attempt to gain control of a situation they cannot yet control. As the group struggles to understand the upward movement of the pole, listen to the communication within the group and watch for conflict that develops. Is there blaming? Is there competition? Who begins to negotiate and take control of the situation? Who attempts to get everyone moving in the same direction? How do people respond to their efforts? What processes do they develop for getting control of the energy in the group?

Groups typically try a variety of techniques for improving the quality of their performance. In general, the first step is to halt any upward movement. Higher-level skills are certainly required to induce downward movement. Actually lowering the pole anywhere close to the ground is excellent teamwork. One of the most efficient techniques for helping your staff succeed at this activity is to invite them away from the pole for discussion. They remain in this position until they are ready for another attempt. This distance from the problem allows them to focus on the actions of the group, rather than the physics of the pole itself.

Some techniques exhibited by successful teams include minimizing the number of fingers touching the pole (to minimize the upward force). If each person only uses one finger instead of two to support the pole, a more favorable balance of force is possible.

Once your staff have successfully caused the pole to move in a downward direction, ask them some of these questions:

- What happened to the pole?
- What happened to the group as they tried to reach the goal?
- Was there any blaming and frustration expressed?
- How did you overcome the conflict that developed in the group?
- How did you come to an agreement about how to solve the problem?
- Whose job is it to guide the group to resolve their conflicts so they can reach their goal?
- Who was making the pole go up?
- Was it intentional?
- How did you get control so the pole started moving in the right direction?
- What did it take to get control of the group's energy so it was moving in the direction you wanted it to?

- How is this like our staff in the first few weeks of working together?
- How do we get staff behavior moving in the right direction?
- How do we get participant behavior moving in the right direction?

An interesting variation of this activity is to use a lightweight hula hoop instead of a pole. The facilitator stands in the center of the hoop to begin the activity, pressing downward as participants place a finger or two below the hoop and press upward with a slight pressure. Initial attempts at this circular version of the Helium Stick typically have the same result as the linear version.

BOX 4.15

In the Helium Stick activity, I have actually had some participants inspect the pole to look for hidden wires or ask me if the pole has some magical qualities that make it rise. Perhaps magnets are hidden in the ceiling panels! It is not uncommon to hear a frustrated participant say, *"Why are you guys going up?"* even as that person's hands are the highest in the group. It is also common for folks in one area to blame folks in other areas: *"It must be the people on the end,"* say the folks in the middle. *"It is the tall people,"* say the short people, and so on.

The secret to success in this activity is getting everyone in the group to focus on the desired outcome (moving the pole in a downward direction), slowing down to get control of the process, and coordination of the entire group—exactly the same skills that will help your staff succeed at many future tasks! The Helium Stick is an excellent activity for identifying which members of your staff are likely to step up and take control when a situation seems out of control.

The C5 Youth Foundation's summer staff supervisor training program includes materials from the book *Super Staff Supervision,* by Michael Brandwein. The Helium Stick is a great activity to introduce material from *Path 4: Managing Undesirable Staff Behavior in Positive Ways.* After participating in this activity, supervisors have the opportunity to discuss their assumptions about staff, when they exhibit undesirable behaviors. It is easy to assume that staff behaviors are all intentional, but in many cases mistakes result from letting the energy of the first week of employment carry them in directions that aren't really productive. How do we deal with these behaviors differently than *intentional behaviors?* What should our expectations and processes be early in their work experience, compared to later, and how can establishing a consistent coaching process help staff use their energy appropriately? As a result of these discussions, a weekly coaching process has been established between supervisors and staff.

Clare-Marie Hannon

🔲 29. Alphabet Soup

Here is an activity that explores continuous improvement, reducing errors and teamwork. It is one of only a few team activities that you can successfully repeat

multiple times and sustain the active engagement of your participants each time. In fact, the energy of your staff will increase as their performance continues to improve.

The name for this activity, *Alphabet Soup,* comes from the appearance of random letters floating in a circular bowl. You can create your own soup bowl with 26 index cards (printed with the letters A through Z) and sufficient rope to create a circle approximately 20 feet (6 meters) in diameter. You'll also need another shorter rope to use as a start/finish line. You can use the numbers 1 though

30 instead of letters for this activity, although *Number Soup* doesn't quite have the same ring to it. The artistic collection of number cards shown in the photograph include the numbers 1 though 30, created from different shapes, fonts, and languages (for a multicultural version).

The challenge in this activity is for a team to race from the starting line to the circle, touch all the cards in ascending order, and return to their starting location as quickly and as error-free as possible. Here are the basic rules:

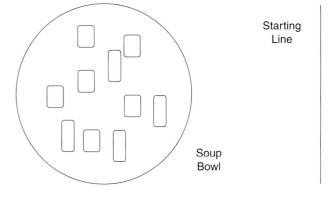

Starting Line

Soup Bowl

1. Time begins when the first person crosses the starting line and ends when the last person returns.
2. Cards must be touched in ascending order.
3. A five-second penalty is assessed for any of the following three errors:
   - Having more than one person in the bowl at a time. Imagine that the walls of the soup bowl extend upward from the circular rope perimeter. Anyone reaching into this bowl, or even pointing over this boundary, is in the bowl. If one person is standing in the bowl and another person reaches over the line to point at a letter card, this is an error. If two people point over the line while another person is standing in the bowl, this counts as two errors (10 seconds of penalty time).
   - Touching a letter card out of order constitutes an error (five-second penalty).
   - Touching the perimeter rope of the soup bowl constitutes an error (five-second penalty).

4. The total time for each round is a combination of the time required PLUS the total time penalties. A 60-second completion time plus 10 errors (5 seconds each) would create a total time of 110 seconds.

5. The cards, rope boundary, and start/finish line positions are fixed and cannot be moved.

There are a variety of techniques that are possible for the successful and timely completion of this task. Some groups choose to have every participant touch at least one card. Some groups select one *runner* who touches the cards in order, while other team members assist with verbal directions.

Before each round, invite teams to establish a time goal for themselves. When finished, compare this estimate to the actual performance. In addition to setting time goals, encourage teams to establish quality standards to minimize errors. As part of this quality management, encourage teams to inspect their own errors, rather than using a facilitator to do so. This simple act places the responsibility for error accounting and reduction with the participants rather than with an outside observer.

If multiple groups are participating in this activity, allow each team to observe the performance of all groups. This technique will typically increase the inclusion of best practices from other groups, and produce an even more dramatic reduction in errors and time performance.

An Interesting Variation of Alphabet Soup

One of the more interesting variations of the Alphabet Soup initiative involves everyone in the group moving simultaneously. In this version, one letter card is randomly placed for each member of the group. Every member of the team begins by stepping on a single card. Each person must move sequentially from their card around the soup bowl until they arrive back at their starting position. For example, if a total of twelve people are present, the letters A through L would be used. A person starting at letter F would need to touch G, H, I, J, K, L, A, B, C, D and E in order, before returning to the letter F position.

Time is measured from when the first person moves until the last person reaches the starting position. Errors consist of any person bumping into another person (absolutely no contact is allowed), anyone touching a letter out of sequence, or anyone touching the rope boundary for the soup bowl. This version of Alphabet Soup is a bit more realistic to the work environment of many organizations. Everyone needs to know where they each fit into the grand plan and where everyone else is at any given time.

30. The PVC Network

Here is a higher-level challenge that will require many of the skills that a high-performing work team possesses, including communication, problem solving, resource management, creativity, and teamwork.

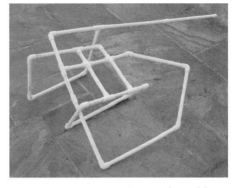

Using a collection of PVC tubes and connectors, groups of four to six participants are asked to create a complete interconnected structure so that no openings (holes) are left.

Some groups use a space station analogy (there can be no open doors in outer space), or perhaps a plumbing system analogy (no leaks).

The goal is for each group to successfully complete their structure and then analyze the performance of their team by themselves at the completion of the project. Although the challenge of successfully completing this task is sufficient enough, the real opportunity in this activity is to provide a high-performing team with a project that they can accomplish by themselves, including a self-review of their performance at the completion of the project. By definition, this is exactly what a high-performing self-directed work team can do.

In the Ready-to-Copy section of this book, you'll find a description of this activity, followed by a full page of staff debriefing questions for each group to discuss once they have completed the challenge (or time has run out).

The PVC tubes and connectors shown here are Teamplay Tubes™, created by Dr. Jim Cain. You can purchase this collection (and instructions for more than a dozen teambuilding activities with these PVC tubes and connectors) from Training Wheels, Inc. at www.training-wheels.com, or by calling (888) 553-0147.

As part of a staff-training program for a cellular phone company in northern Italy, a king-size version of Teamplay Tubes was created. This is a great example of how you can super-size a puzzle for large-group problem solving.

Notes

31. Wah!

For those moments when your staff training needs a bit more energy or when you've had plenty of work and not enough play, here is a fast-moving and simply wonderful game that will re-energize your staff. It helps to deliver the instructions for this activity with the authority and attitude of a Samurai warrior.

Start with eight to twelve people standing in a close circle. Instruct your group to stand in *Wah* position (feet slightly spread like the letter A, and palms together facing towards the center of the circle). All movements in this game happen in groups of three. On the count of *one*, the leader points (with palms together) toward another person and says, "Wah!"

On the count of *two*, that person (grateful to be chosen to receive the Wah) raises their arms straight up (like a tree), palms together, and says, "Wah!"

And on the count of *three*, the people on each side of the "tree" pretend to be lumberjacks and chop at the midsection of the tree (noncontact of course), and say, "Wah!"

At this point, the second person (whose hands are still raised in tree position), has the Wah, and quickly passes it to someone new (on the count of one) and the game continues.

Anyone who fails to correctly perform the required motion, or fails to say, "Wah!" with just the right amount of attitude and energy, or at the required time is out and leaves the circle. Play until you reach the last three players.

If you prefer a nonelimination version of this game, play with several circles near each other. When a person is out of one circle, they can join any other circle.

BOX 4.16

The graph shown here illustrates the concept of an educational continuum (based loosely on the work of M. Banks, 1972) where the *y*-axis shows the degree of freedom (or conversely the degree of external constraint) and the *x*-axis shows a variety of activities and the structure they require. The origin of the *x*-axis is activity that is totally unstructured. This is where you'll find creative play without rules or boundaries like self expression and movement in zero gravity. The far end of the *x*-axis is activity that requires the highest degree of structure, rules, regulations, guidelines, and constraint. Here you'll find government regulated technology, surgical operations, and the like. Somewhere in the middle, between play and work, resides the world of education and training (which in itself has a continuum of freedom and constraint). While certain job-related training is no doubt very structured, there are also training techniques that fall well to the left on the educational continuum.

So why does a discussion about structure, work, and play belong on a page with one of the most playful activities in this book? The answer is quite simple—balance. There are no doubt times in your staff-training plans when you'll need to traverse a variety of topics that fall well in the required list of training components. Activities like *Wah!* help you balance those moments with free play. And if you think there's no way you have time for

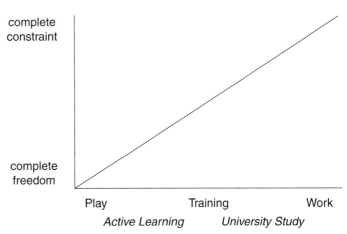

such play when there are so many things to cover in today's schedule, consider this: The chances of your staff actually paying attention and retaining all the highly structured and obviously *required* subject matter are higher if you balance that time with other activities from the less-constrained side of the educational continuum. Consider it an experiment. The next time you have a staff-training program with an overload of structured requirements, introduce something from the less-structured side of the educational continuum and see if that balance improves the quality and retention of the information you present.

Here's one example of how this can be done. Kurt Podeszwa of Camp For All in Texas has a unique way of teaching his staff the highly structured and required information related to child abuse each year. This session is mandatory in Texas for all staff that work with youth. There is even a formal test that must be successfully completed for this state requirement. Kurt helps his staff prepare for this session with a game-show format of questions and answers that successfully balances the highly structured side of training with a more playfully structured study format. Kurt's activity is both respectful of the material content and very effective as a staff training tool. Balance is achieved, and not surprisingly, 100 percent of the staff pass the required examination every time.

So the next time you have a full afternoon of structured training planned for your staff, teach them a quick game of Wah! It's all about the balance.

32. Nose Jousting

Although the phrase *meaningful* probably doesn't apply to this next activity, don't be fooled by its playful nature. Nose Jousting is a terrific way to instantly boost the enthusiasm of your group, help your staff stretch their comfort zones, and to promote good sportsmanship.

Begin by providing all participants with a piece of masking tape. Instruct them to fold this tape into a circle, sticky-side out, and place it on their nose. The challenge begins with two opponents facing each other. They make nose-to-nose contact with the tape on their noses, and as they pull away, one person will "win" the round by capturing both pieces of masking tape.

The winner is allowed to reaffix the tape to their nose between rounds. The losing opponent then becomes the cheering section for the champion, and places their hands on their opponent's shoulders, chanting their name as they take on other opponents. When a challenger beats a player with many members of their cheering section attached, they *all* become the cheering section for the new champion. The competition continues until a final champion wins (complete with a large glob of masking tape on their nose!) This activity is loud, boisterous, and just plain fun.

While the act of pressing your nose against another person's nose may be a bit outside of most folks' comfort zone, there is a higher purpose to the fine art of nose jousting. The moment a person is defeated, they quickly become the cheering section for their champion. Many people quickly forget that they have lost a previous round, and enjoy chanting the name of their champion. Games like this promote good sportsmanship and fairplay—two qualities of which the world could use a bit more of these days.

One Big Brothers/Big Sisters organization uses their version of nose jousting to discuss comfort zones and trust between bigs and littles in their program. In the first round, participants place one piece of masking tape on the knuckles of their middle and ring fingers and play the game using only their hands. In the second round, they progress from hand movements to the traditional form of nose jousting mentioned above. This nose-to-nose version obviously requires some people to step outside their personal comfort zones. As a result, a wonderful discussion is created about how to make the big/little relationship successful, and not push too quickly into the comfort zone of your brother or sister.

This organization must be doing something right. The success rate between Big Brothers and Big Sisters and their young partners is over 90 percent. They have also demonstrated how to use a playful activity to introduce an important and necessary discussion topic as part of their training program.

◼ 33. Interference

Here is a classic communication activity that explores the relationship between those sending a message, those receiving it, and those things that interfere with this process. This activity will create valuable discussions within your staff about overcoming the interference that can minimize the information being received.

Begin by dividing the available space into three segments, and mark the space between these segments with a line.

Senders   Interferers   Receivers

Next, divide the group into three equally sized subgroups. The first group members are the *senders,* the middle group members are the *interferers,* and the final group members are the *receivers.* The object is for the senders to verbally transmit a message to the receivers. The interferers are busy, however, attempting to block the message. Cycle through this activity three times, with each group taking on each of the three roles (i.e., in round two, senders become interferers, interferers become receivers, and receivers become senders). Senders are given 30 seconds to communicate their message. No physical contact between team members is allowed. After 30 seconds, the facilitator asks the receivers to repeat the message.

Once every member of the group has participated in each of the three roles (sender, interferer, and receiver), a review or debriefing session can be used to discuss the following questions. Which role was easiest to play, and why? What techniques did your group utilize to be most effective in your role? Who are the senders and receivers of your messages at work? What things create interference with your messages?

Here are a few concise messages to transmit during this activity. Facilitators can share this information with the senders by whispering it to them or giving them an index card with the following information:

Message Number 1   In order to listen, you must first become quiet.
Message Number 2   Somewhere in the forest, there is a tree that longs to be a ship.
Message Number 3   The best things in life, are not things.

Not surprisingly, the interferer role is one of the most fun to play in this activity. These folks have the unique responsibility to disrupt the message, distract the senders and receivers, and basically add a great deal of chaos, noise, and confusion to the communication process.

As a means of presenting this communication model in an even more physical frame of reference, try this variation. Create an activity space with three zones. Invite one third of the group to stand in the top zone, and another third to stand in the bottom zone. We'll get to the remaining third of the group in a few minutes. The senders (in the top zone here) are asked to wear a label or nametag with the word *Sender* written on it. Those in the bottom zone are asked to wear a label with the word *Receiver* easily visible. Each sender is provided with a soft throwable object (such as a stuffed animal or ball). This object has the word *Message* written on it.

Initially, each sender finds a partner on the receiving line and practices throwing the message successfully to this partner. The goal is to be successful in making sure your partner receives the message every time it is thrown. During this time, the remaining third group can observe the senders and receivers working together, and identify what they are doing to be most effective.

Next, invite both groups to sit down in their zone. Senders again transmit their message to the receivers. But discuss the fact that the senders can see that a message was received, but not confirm that the *right* message was received. What is missing is some needed feedback, so invite the receiver to transmit the message back to the sender. The sender can now confirm that this was the correct message. This feedback component is critical for two-way communication.

But transmitting information isn't always this easy, is it? Sometimes things interfere with our communications. For the last third of the group, provide each person with a cardboard sign that says *interference* on it. Invite them to stand in the middle zone between the two groups. In this stage of the activity, these interferers will attempt to disrupt the message being transmitted between the senders and receivers. Physical contact between the interferers and senders or receivers is discouraged, but blocking the path (even with their sign) is possible. Have the senders and receivers attempt to send their message back and forth several times, and note the amount of times the message arrives successfully.

Discuss the following questions: *What happened to our messages? What did the sender and receiver do to successfully communicate? What kind of interference occurred that kept messages from being successfully received?*

Next, replace the throwable messages with some of the verbal messages listed earlier. Invite the senders and receivers to discuss how they plan to make sure their messages arrive accurately. Provide each sender 30 seconds to "transmit" the message and then ask each receiver to discuss the content of the message. *Was the message successfully received? Was the received message altered in any way? What strategy did the senders use? What strategy did the receivers use?*

Finally, invite participants to identify four kinds of interference they could experience in their work environment, four techniques they can use to be better senders, and four things they can do to be better receivers.

BOX 4.18

This is a wonderful activity because it gives the verbal concept of communication a very physical frame of reference. Often, staff members *check out* during a training session as soon as the word *communication* is mentioned. They either think they know all there is to know about communication or have given up trying to figure out what is being discussed. It is often very easy to identify in any given conversation who are the senders, the receivers, and the interferers. Activities like Interference generate energy and invite groups to think creatively about how to improve communication.

One of the first times I facilitated this activity, I had a tech-savvy group of high-school-age trainees. As soon as I said go, one staff member pulled out a cell phone and called a person on the receivers' side and gave them the message. I admit, my first response to this was, *"Hey, you can't do that!"* But this was surely a clear case of generational difference in the tools we use to communicate. In many training and working environments, cell phone usage during work hours is either forbidden or severely limited. But technology defines the preferred method of communication for many younger staff members. This incident created a great opportunity to discuss the benefits and limitations of a wide variety of technological enhancements to communication and how those tools fit into the work environment.

Clare-Marie Hannon

BOX 4.19

I first learned this activity from Tom Heck. Tom is an innovative and thoughtful practitioner of adventure-based and active learning. You can find out more about Tom and his work at www.teachmeteamwork.com.

Jim Cain

Notes

34. Object Retrieval

This is a great activity for exploring both creative problem solving and resourcefulness with your staff. It is effective for framing discussion around the importance of finding creative solutions using only the resources at hand. It is also an outstanding activity for reinforcing multiple correct solutions to a problem, encouraging your staff to find not only the first acceptable solution, but others as well.

You'll need a variety of simple props for this activity, including string, rope, rubber bands, a bucket or milk crate, a plastic tablecloth, roll of masking tape, wooden dowels, sections of PVC pipe and connectors, and other things you probably have in your toolbox, garage, or basement. Begin by creating a 13 foot (4 meter)-diameter circle, using rope, masking tape, or sidewalk chalk. Balance an object in the center of the circle on a small platform, such as a beach ball on a tin can. In the case of the photograph shown here, two towers were erected and multiple items were presented for retrieval to create additional challenges for the group.

Challenge the group to retrieve the object from the center of the circle three times in thirty minutes using three *fundamentally* different approaches, without allowing anyone or anything to touch the ground inside the circle. Set expectations with the group that the activity ends upon the third successful retrieval of the object, or the first time someone (or something) touches the ground within the circle. These expectations will make quality performance equally important to creative thinking.

For safety, follow these guidelines. Avoid tying or tightly wrapping any rope or string around any part of the body. Anyone to be lifted during an attempt should be carefully spotted by the facilitator and additional staff. If you are unfamiliar with spotting techniques, encourage your staff to use a method that will not require lifting any member of the team. Inspect all knots for security. Discourage any technique that involves running or diving. These are unsafe and typically unsuccessful.

Reviewing this activity with your staff can focus on issues of time and resource management, working successfully as part of a team, dividing an assignment into smaller parts, creativity, safety, and (hopefully) celebrating success together as a team.

BOX 4.20

While facilitating a group of teachers one day, I was surprised when our debriefing conversation turned from a general discussion about teamwork to a very specific discussion around the concept of connecting with youth. The object in the center of our retrieval activity became a metaphor for children. This team of teachers focused on two key issues. First, they acknowledged that their job was to find ways to connect with each and every child. Second, they needed to be successful in their work because the consequence of failure was unacceptable. Their rally cry for the rest of the session and the rest of their school year became *no room for error!* Since that time, whenever I use this activity for a staff training session, I deliberately frame the activity around this metaphor.

Dave Knobbe

Notes

35. Texas Leghorn (Alaskan Baseball)

This activity is sure to increase the heart rate of everyone in your staff. In just a few minutes of play, you can reenergize your entire staff, and have fun while doing it!

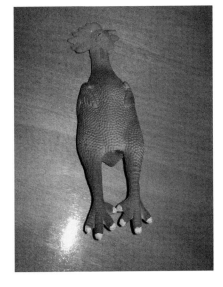

You'll need a soft, throwable object for this activity. Balls are not recommended as they tend to roll, but nearly any other soft object is fine (stuffed animals, dog toys, etc.) The name *Texas Leghorn* comes from a group of youth workers in Texas that chose to use a rubber chicken as the flying object of choice. It is our favorite, too.

Begin by dividing your staff into teams of six to ten players. For this explanation, we'll imagine that you have two teams of ten players. One team tosses the rubber chicken as far as they can. This same team then forms a tight circle, while the chicken thrower begins to run laps around the other members of this team. With every lap the chicken thrower makes, their team counts loudly, *"one, two, three. . . ."*

While this is happening, the second team races to pick up the rubber chicken. As soon as the first person from their team grabs the chicken, the rest of the team lines up behind them. The chicken grabber then passes the chicken between their legs to the person behind them. This person passes the chicken over their head to the person behind them. This pattern of *between the legs* and *over the head* continues until the last person receives the chicken. This team then yells loudly, "Done!" and the last person throws the chicken as far as they can (and typically away from the direction of the other team).

At this point, the process reverses, and the second team is now in a tight circle, with their chicken thrower running laps around them, while the first team is racing after the chicken and passing it over their heads and between their legs. The first team to score a cumulative total of 15 laps (points) wins. But by this point, everyone will be breathing hard and laughing hysterically.

BOX 4.21

After only one or two rounds of this activity, you'll have elevated the heart rate of every member of your staff. For those moments when you only have time for a brief break in your staff training, this activity will give you the most elevated heart rates and attention levels for only the cost of a rubber chicken.

■ 36. Vision Walk

The Vision Walk is an example of a truly challenging minimal-prop activity with tremendous impact if the group succeeds. It is an excellent activity to help your staff clarify their vision for the future. It also illustrates the importance of having a plan in place to get where you want to go.

It is important to sequence this activity appropriately in your staff-training plan. If used too early in the training process (while the group is still developing), the challenge level of this activity is likely to overwhelm your staff. Once your staff have established trust and successfully solved several team challenges together, this activity will empower them with a sense of direction and confidence that they can accomplish what at first might seem impossible.

Equipment needs for this activity are one blindfold per person, one segment of rope 50 to 100 feet (15–30 meters) long, and one bandana. This collection of equipment is appropriate for staff groups of approximately six to twenty people. If you have more than this number, consider splitting the group into two or more separate groups. You'll also need a large area of open space—flat and grassy with no obstacles is ideal.

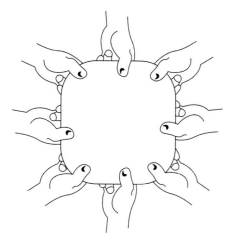

Begin at a clearly designated starting point. This point represents the present. Lead a discussion about the group's vision. Create meaning around an object such as a bandana by passing it around the group and having each person share their vision for their future as they hold the object. Invite each person to grasp the object simultaneously, clarify that the object represents the collective vision of the group, and that at the successful close of the activity, they will again be gathered around the object with each person holding part of the bandana.

Lead the group to a spot 100 yards or more from the starting point and set the single bandana in the middle of the available space or tie it at a reasonable height from the branch of an overhanging tree. Explain that this point represents the location where they will realize their future.

The group has a significant challenge. To return to the starting location (with sight) and move from that position to the bandana while everyone is blindfolded. Encourage your staff to create a plan that *guarantees* they can be successful.

Allow 15 to 25 minutes for the group to walk back to the starting point and create their plan. Be sure to share the following information with them:

- *All* members are blindfolded from the time they leave the starting point until they recover the object.
- The group may not mark their path in advance, and they may use only one additional resource: the length of rope.
- The group may remove their blindfolds only when all members of the group are touching the bandana representing their collective vision.

 If you happen to use bandanas as blindfolds for this activity, choose a color different from the one retrieved by the group. At the completion of the activity, you can allow participants to take their bandana as a keepsake token for this activity.

Notes

▪ 37. Moving with Purpose (Playing Card Line-up)

This activity demonstrates that group performance is enhanced by individuals who share a common vision, work within the organizational structure by respecting specific boundaries and norms, understand their role and adapt accordingly, and who perform their assigned role efficiently and purposefully. When these contributing factors are optimized, a group's performance is likely to exceed even their own wildest expectations.

This activity requires a deck of ordinary playing cards and a stopwatch. You'll need one card per person. If you happen to have more than 52 staff members present, you can add random cards from another deck to reach the required total. For smaller groups, you can either take the same number of random cards from each suit, or reduce the number of suits from four to three or two as necessary. You'll need at least 6 cards per suit. This activity works best with groups of twenty or more.

The challenge of this activity is for the entire group to arrange themselves in order as directed by the facilitator, as quickly as possible. In each successive round, encourage the group to improve their process and lower their total time.

Begin by distributing one card per person (face down). Participants hold their card in their hands and are instructed not to look at their card until asked to do so. At this point, the facilitator provides information about the line-up procedure. For example, "Line up in number order with people holding the same card suit as you." Once line-up directions are given, and the facilitator says, "Go!" participants can look at their card, and timing begins. When everyone in the group has arranged themselves in the appropriate order, and they all clap once in unison, timing stops. This time is then reported to the group. After each round, participants exchange cards (face down) at least three times with other participants. In between rounds, participants are encouraged to discuss their strategy and make suggestions for improvement.

Although this collection of information may seem minimal, it is generally sufficient. Encourage the group to assist their own members who may have additional questions or comments. Conduct several rounds with identical line-up procedures, followed by some variations. For example:

Rounds 1, 2, and 3:	Line up in number order by similar card suit.
Round 4:	Without looking at your card, place it to your forehead, and line up in number order by similar card suit.
Round 5:	Line up in number order with people who have the same color suit (red or black).
Round 6:	Line up alphabetically by suit (Eight comes alphabetically before Five, etc.).

Because this activity can be performed with a very large number of participants, the debriefing process can be challenging. Rather than reviewing with the entire group, encourage small groups of approximately five people to discuss the performance of the group through the various rounds. This technique will enable a much larger quantity of people to voice their comments than is possible in one large group. Additional debriefing questions can include the following:

- What did it take to build an efficient process for getting the job done?
- What obstacles did you encounter during the activity?
- How do we overcome such obstacles in the future?
- What are the similarities between this activity and our future work as a team?
- What do we expect from each other as we move forward?
- What is the most significant take-away from this activity?

Moving with Purpose can be a fascinating activity to observe with very large groups. As your staff work to more clearly define both the task and their individual responsibilities, they begin to move more efficiently. In most cases, the time required for the group to complete the task will improve dramatically. Once the group has perfected the process and individuals understand their role in this activity, their confidence improves. This can be said for their regular job duties as well!

In the end, your staff will share a common vision, understand their role in operating within the structure and order set by the facilitator, be adaptable to change, and perform their role efficiently.

BOX 4.23

For even more team activities with playing cards, see the book *Playing with a Full Deck—52 Team Activities Using a Deck of Cards* by Michelle Cummings, 2007, Kendall/Hunt Publishers, Dubuque, Iowa, ISBN 978-0-7575-4094-3.

And watch the Teamwork & Teamplay website for more information about the book, *It's All in the Cards!* by Jim Cain and Michelle Cummings. This book contains 101 playful, interactive, challenging, thought-provoking, conversational, educational, valuable, and fun things to do with ordinary index cards and playing cards. Visit www.teamworkandteamplay.com for more information.

Notes

38. Hieroglyphics

Here is a linguistic challenge that you can share with your staff, working in groups of three. As with most of the activities in this book, you have the option of using this activity purely as a fun way to encourage your staff to work together, or you can use this activity to open the door to a discussion concerning how members of the group find the answers to critical questions they have. Where can they go when they don't have the knowledge they need to complete a task?

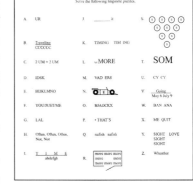

Begin this activity in groups of three. After a few minutes of problem solving, invite two groups to work together (doubling the brain power).

You'll find a full-page version of hieroglyphics in the Ready-to-Copy section of this book.

Answers

A	Half an Hour	B	Traveling Over Seas	C	Forum
D	Mixed Up Kids	E	Water (H2O)	F	Just Between You and Me
G	All Mixed Up	H	More Often than Not	I	Long Time No See (no C)
J	Blanket	K	Split Second Timing	L	A Little Bit More
M	Space Invaders	N	Eraser	O	Jack in the Box
P	That's Beside the Point	Q	Tuna Fish	R	Room for One More
S	Tennis Balls	T	The Start of Something Big	U	Cyclones
V	Going on a Double Date	W	Banana Split	X	Quit Following Me
		Y	Love at First Sight	Z	A Bad Spell of Weather

For a more active version of this activity, instead of placing multiple hieroglyphics on a single page, try placing each hieroglyphic on an index card and then scattering these puzzles around the training room, building, or even around the property. Teams can then exercise their bodies as well as their minds as they solve these challenges. You can also use these hieroglyphics as part of a geo-caching, letterboxing, scavenger hunt, or orienteering circuit.

BOX 4.24

Here is another technique that promotes teamwork in this activity. Invite each group to send one ambassador to meet at a central location. Ambassadors are asked to share their knowledge and also request the answers to those hieroglyphics their group has not yet solved. Limit the amount of time the ambassadors meet. Sixty seconds should be about right.

■ 39. Loop the Loop

Here is an activity with a physical component to help your staff look critically at the process of change and adaptation. Loop the Loop is a sequence of four activities, each of which requires the group to adapt from their previous experiences.

By performing this series of activities sequentially, you'll notice that the success of the group is affected by the desire of some staff members to keep doing things the old way rather than adapting to a new and changing set of requirements. Staff members must determine when learning from experience when previous knowledge is useful and when it is best to approach a situation with a fresh perspective. This is also an excellent activity for reinforcing the nine-step problem-solving process introduced in the activity Inside/Out.

You'll need several hula hoops and one Raccoon Circle for this activity.

Round One—Circle the Circle

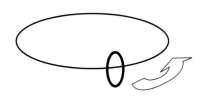

Invite your entire group to stand in a circle and hold hands. The facilitator should place their hand through the hula hoop as they join hands with the rest of the group. The task is now to pass the hoop around the circle so that each person passes through it, without breaking continuous hand contact. Encourage your staff to help each other. For an additional challenge, you can pass multiple hula hoops in the same direction, or pass two different sizes of hula hoops in opposite directions.

Round Two—Circle the Circle Times Two

Now introduce a second, slightly smaller hula hoop to the group. In this round, one hoop will travel clockwise around the group, the second hoop will travel counter-clockwise.

Round Three—Circle the Circle with a Raccoon Circle

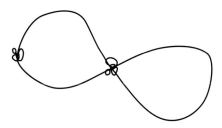

Replace the two hula hoops with a single knotted Raccoon Circle. Tie an additional knot in the Raccoon Circle to create the figure-eight pattern shown. The challenge in this round is to pass one loop of the Raccoon Circle to the right around the circle, and the other loop at the same time to the left. You'll notice that more members of the group are active in this round than previous rounds.

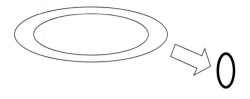

Round Four—The Amoeba

Divide your group in half and ask them to create two concentric circles. This arrangement looks surprisingly like an amoeba, with an interior nucleus and an exterior cell wall. Next hold the flexible Raccoon Circle hoop for the group, and ask them to "jump" though it.

Inform them than an amoeba will flow when moving from place to place. Caution them that at no time can the interior nucleus of the amoeba extend beyond the exterior cell wall. Also inform the group that after the amoeba has started through the Raccoon Circle hoop the facilitator will let go.

Groups typically struggle with the similarities between these activities, even though they require the individuals to change their behavior in order to be successful. The experiences of passing the hoop around the circle influences the ability of your staff to understand and plan for another task that appears similar, but is in fact different.

Debriefing topics for this activity can include discussion related to change, learning from past experiences, adaptation to a changing environment, and working together as a team.

One variation that I enjoy when passing hula hoops around a circle is to use four or five at a time. Challenge your group to pass these hoops in the same direction, while keeping them together, and have each person, while passing through the hoops, share some interesting and fun personal details about themselves. For some people, this is like patting your head and rubbing your stomach at the same time. It is a multitasking activity that generates plenty of laughter.

Dave Knobbe

Notes

40. Stretching the Limit

This creative problem-solving activity is made even more valuable by dividing the total time available into two separate pieces—ten minutes of planning time and one minute for execution. This single activity explores five useful staff skills, including: problem solving, finding the resources you need, teamwork, advanced planning, and time management. One activity—five valuable skills, and plenty to talk about after the time has run out.

The basic challenge of Stretching the Limit is to create a continuous line from the anchor or starting point toward a specific goal in one direction. Participants are encouraged to use any nearby object that can help them extend their reach. This can include not only those items in their proximity, but also such things as shoelaces, belts, and other creative extensions. You can provide some typical extension devices in this activity, such as rope, broomsticks, chairs, extension cords (of course!), and other objects you find nearby. You'll also need a container of some sort (bucket, trash can, bowl, paper bag, or cardboard box), some paper, and a few pens. Finally, you'll need to conduct this activity in an area with plenty of open space and room to expand.

Begin this activity at the starting location by inviting members of the group to discuss a personal goal they have for the near future. Ask them to write this goal on an index card and place it into the container. After all written goals have been contributed, place the container a significant distance away from the group.

Inform the group that their challenge will be to build a continuous line from this starting location (point out a specific anchor point, such as a tree or other fixed object) to our goals. For the next ten minutes, you can verbally plan your efforts, and then you'll have exactly one minute to accomplish this task. During the one minute of execution time, you can gather any nearby resources to assist you in reaching your goals, but again, you can only gather these items during the execution time. Encourage your staff to utilize any suitable resource, but prohibit the destruction of any resource that could be adversely affected by participation in this activity (i.e. branches from a nearby tree, removing the legs from a table, etc.).

Groups are challenged to use the ten minutes of planning time only for verbal conversation. Encourage them to plan carefully. If staff members begin to gather resources, ask them to focus on the planning component, *not* the resource identification and retrieval component at this time.

When the planning time has elapsed, the group will have one minute to complete the task.

After time has run out, gather your group together to discuss their performance. Were they successful in completing a continuous line from the starting point to their goals? Was their planning process sufficient? What resources were creatively used? Were there any situations that did not happen as planned? If this group was asked to perform this same task again, at night, without lights, what would they do differently? During their original problem-solving planning process, what was the most valuable thing they discussed?

For many organizations, planning can take a significant portion of the entire project timeline. Thorough planning and a quick and successful execution of the plan are valuable skills indeed.

As a facilitator, I have learned some valuable lessons when incorporating the kinds of activities presented in this book. You will, too! The good news is, we tend to get better at the things we practice. Each time I lead one of these activities, I see opportunities for improving not only the quality of the activity, but also the conversations I can have with the group at the completion of each activity.

I learned a valuable lesson with the activity Stretching the Limit. Prior to dividing the time for this activity into two segments, I typically introduced the challenge and allowed the group to plan and execute this activity on their own. What I discovered is that the individuals near the starting point (or anchor end) of the line do not have nearly the level of involvement or energy as their teammates farther down the line. It can be a bit boring just holding a rope while your teammates are busy at the far end of the line. By using two different time limits, and encouraging both advanced planning and quick execution, I noticed that participants were much more engaged throughout the activity, and that the overall quality of the activity was improved.

You are invited, and, yes, even encouraged, to safely modify any of the activities in this book to help achieve your desired outcome. In fact, when I was first new at facilitating activities, I would purposefully change something in each of the activities I did, just to see if it was better than the last time I used that activity. Adapt. Change. Alter. Evolve. That is what turns a good activity into a great one.

Jim Cain

Notes

▪ 41. 10 × 10 × 10: A Leadership Challenge Activity

This leadership challenge activity was co-created by Dr. Jim Cain and Clare-Marie Hannon as part of the C5 Youth Foundation's leadership curriculum. This activity was

part of the final exam session, after participants in the program were familiar with a wide range of leadership skills. As such, the review of this activity can incorporate all of the previous leadership lessons. Extensive debriefing and reviewing examples are provided at the end of this activity (based on the 16 separate leadership topics explored as part of the C5 Leadership program).

The basic challenge is for a leader to assist their group in moving 10 people, 10 feet in 10 minutes. This challenge is simple to explain, but not so simple to complete in the 10 minutes allotted. A script for the activity leader is presented in the Read-to-Copy section of this book.

You'll need a total of 10 participants in this activity, plus one leader and at least one observer. The facilitator should choose a member of the group to lead this activity. This selection should not be a random or volunteer choice, but someone who has exhibited leadership capabilities during previous activities and who has a reasonable chance of completing the assignment successfully. Volunteers are accepted for those actually standing on the walking boards. Any remaining staff members are encouraged to take on the roles of observers.

Begin the set-up for this activity by placing two untied Raccoon Circles 10 feet apart, as shown in the illustration. Next place 11 walking boards in a U-shaped pattern. Invite the leader of the group to stand at the top of the U shape and for 10 members of the team to stand on the boards (with one foot on one board and the other foot on another nearby board).

As stated in the script available in the Ready-to-Copy section of this book, the leader has 10 minutes to get 10 people to move 10 feet using the props provided. This one activity will incorporate a wide variety of leadership topics and themes. One member of the group is selected to be the official leader of the group, ten members complete the task, and remaining team members are chosen to be active observers. Invite these observers to use the 16 leadership themes and questions listed at the end of this activity for observation guidelines while watching the group complete the task.

Here are a few basic rules. Planning time is part of the 10 minutes. The two lines are 10 feet apart. Group members must cross the space between these two lines. Only the wooden boards can touch the ground between the two lines. The team leader will ultimately have to decide how much time to spend planning, leaving sufficient time to complete the task. Practicing behind the starting line is allowed and encouraged. Any mistakes made behind the starting line have no consequences. Only the people who cross the starting line on any particular board are allowed to touch that board during the completion of the task. Only one person at a time is allowed to touch any one of the ropes attached to each board (this encourages contact with each other instead). The job is done (and timing stops) when the group has crossed the finish line and calls time. All questions from the group should be directed toward the leader (not the facilitator).

The following graphics illustrate a typical starting position for this activity. One of the more interesting opportunities in this activity is for the group to modify their initial starting position.

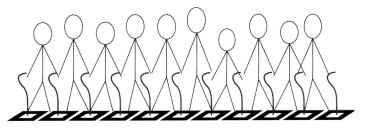

Starting Line (everyone begins *behind* this line)

Finish Line (we are done when *everyone* crosses this line)

Equipment

You can make your own walking boards for this activity using three-quarter-inch-thick (19mm) thick plywood squares and 60 inch (152 cm) long segments of flat webbing (like a short Raccoon Circle).

You can also purchase this equipment ready-made from Training Wheels, Inc. at www.training-wheels.com, or (888) 553-1047.

Teachable Moments and Leadership Reviewing Themes

Unlike many teambuilding activities, 10 × 10 × 10 was created to specifically reinforce leadership skills. Because of this focus, the leader of the group typically, and often incorrectly, assumes that the rules and goals apply to those completing the task. In fact, the rules apply to *everyone!* The most common error in this activity is that the person providing leadership to the group often breaks the rule that only boards can touch in the space between the two lines. This action alone brings the opportunity to discuss why the leaders thought the rules didn't apply to them.

Walking Board
(12″ × 12″ plywood board with 60 inch rope handle)

In addition, you can use any of the following leadership themes from the C5 Youth Foundation for discussion at the completion of this activity. Choose the ones that make the most sense for the teachable moments that occurred during this task. For example:

1. *Character and core values. Honesty* (Did participants tell if they touched the ground?); *Respect* (Did participants listen to each other and value others' ideas?); *Kindness* (When time began to run out, did participants stress levels, and kindness levels, change?)
2. *Ethics.* Did participants behave ethically? Were they honest and fair in their completion of the task? Did they offer excuses for unethical behavior?
3. *Community service.* Were participants actively involved in the successful completion of the task, or did they fail to contribute in this area? Did the leader lead by example, by command, or by being a servant leader?
4. *Creating your personal model of leadership.* Did the solution look like the one that each person envisioned? Did your own individual performance match your expectations for completing the project? Do you think that each member of the group was moving in the same directions (i.e., had the same idea in mind for solving this problem)?
5. *Appreciating diversity.* Were a variety of ideas and opinions shared during the planning and completion of this project? Was everyone's input valued?
6. *Learning from experience and from failure.* What did you learn from early failures in this project? Did anyone have any experience that helped in the completion of this task? What did the leader learn while trying to get the job done? If a mistake was made, did the members of the group want to give up, or try again? Which mistake was the most valuable when trying to figure out how to complete this task?

7. *Communication skills.* How did the group organize to complete this task? Was this an effective way to work together? How did members of the group communicate while they were trying to finish the task? What body language did you observe during this project? If you were to write a one-sentence headline about this project team, what would you write?

8. *Trust.* What words did you hear that made you think that the members of this group either trusted or did not trust each other during this project?

9. *Positive attitude.* When was the energy level of the group highest? During the first try, second, last? How optimistic were you that the project would be successfully completed on time? What words did you hear that inspired the group? Who said these words? What did the leader do to motivate the members of the group? At the completion of the activity, how did the team members celebrate their accomplishments?

10. *Flexibility to change.* Was it easy for the group to change from working on one idea to another? Were members of the group open-minded about trying different ideas, or not?

11. *Managing conflict, building consensus.* What signs did you see to tell you that collaboration happened during this project? What are the relationships of the members of this team? How can you tell this from their performance during this activity? How did the leader help the members of the group decide on the right technique to begin solving this problem? What happened when a mistake was made? How did the group respond?

12. *Balance.* How did the leader balance the planning and doing time of this project? How well did the leader manage power? Did any members of the group change positions so that their skills would better match the people they were working near? Was there an equal amount of learning and play in this activity? If not, how could a better balance be made? What growing experience did you receive from working on this project?

13. *Goal setting.* Did the team set a goal for itself at the start of the project? Did the team meet their goal? Did they meet their time limit? Did they get the job done? Were some members of the group challenged more than others?

14. *Creative problem solving.* What techniques were tried in this project? How did the group decide which idea to try first? What technique did they use to compare possibilities? Did anyone share an idea from her own personal experience? What resources did the group use to solve the problem? What was the most creative idea? Who in the group demonstrated the most imagination?
15. *Responsibility and accountability.* Did each member of the group contribute to get the job done? Do you think everyone was equally committed to getting the job done? Who's job was it to make sure the problem was solved? How was that accomplished?
16. *Team skills.* Who is more responsible for the results, the leader or the team? What words did you hear that told you how well this team worked together? Did you see anyone teaching someone else how to do something well? How did the leader organize the group? Who, in addition to the leader, helped the team solve the problem? What did they do during this project?

Further Discussion: The Task, Growth, Relationship Model

Organizational wisdom says that there are three things necessary for any group to function well together: a worthy *task,* the chance to *grow* and learn new things, and an opportunity to create and improve *relationships* with others within the group. Groups that have *all* of these three components typically experience a higher-quality work life, have better staff retention, and enjoy their work more than those that do not.

In the activity 10 × 10 × 10, many groups focus only on the task of moving 10 people in 10 minutes a total of 10 feet. If they do not succeed in this task, they sometimes feel like they have failed as a group. But there is much more to this activity than just moving people. If your group learned something valuable while performing this activity, or improved the relationships within the group, that is also something worth celebrating!

Think of the *task, growth, relationship* model as an apple pie, where each component is like an ingredient in the pie. If you have all three, then the pie tastes pretty good. If one (or more) of the ingredients is missing, then the pie isn't very good at all.

Which of these three components does each member of your group have? Are they in equal parts? Or, are some of these ingredients more important than the others? How do you get better at each of these three components? For example, how can you improve your relationships with other members of this group?

How well did your group do in the 10 × 10 × 10 activity with the task? With growing and learning new things? With maintaining and improving the relationships between people in our group?

Leadership is hard. It takes lots of work, and practice to be good at it. What do you know now about working together as a group, that you didn't know before 10 × 10 × 10?

BOX 4.27

If you've enjoyed $10 \times 10 \times 10$ and this style of leadership activities, go to the Teamwork & Teamplay Web site (www.teamworkandteamplay.com) for information about the next publication from Jim Cain and Clare-Marie Hannon, *Exploring Leadership*.

Notes

Ten Activities to Help Your Staff Navigate the Five Stages of Group Development

Forming, Storming, Norming, Performing, and Transforming

Throughout the staff orientation and training process and during the day-to-day development of a work group, team members progress through five well-documented stages of group development. Starting with the orientation and dependence stage, and followed by stages of conflict, group cohesion, functional role-relatedness, and finally adjournment, groups experience a sequentially progressing series of roles and behaviors. Bruce Tuckman of The Ohio State University School of Education first proposed these stages in his now-classic 1965 paper in the *Psychological Bulletin*. Commonly referred to as forming, storming, norming, performing, and adjourning (or transforming), these five stages are necessary, normal, and typical in the development of most groups.

The following paragraphs provide valuable information about each stage. You can help your staff navigate each of these stages by exploring the following activities with them and using the tools and suggestions provided.

The *forming* stage is the polite, get-acquainted, icebreaking stage of group development. This process begins at the moment new staff members first begin to assemble. At this point, members of the group are just trying to identify who's who, and where they fit in. This stage includes forming an atmosphere of safety and acceptance, avoiding controversy, and is filled with guidance and direction from the director, manager, or group leader. Get-acquainted and community-building activities are used in this first stage, where positive staff relationships first begin to form. Structure, organization and an inclusive atmosphere are ideal at this stage.

The second, or *storming,* stage introduces conflict and competition into the formerly safe and pleasant work environment. This stage is typically encountered around week two, when many staff members have reached their limit of sleeplessness. Suddenly, those things that didn't matter begin to matter, and conflicts arise. Staff behavior ranges from silence to domination in this environment, and a director needs to utilize coaching to successfully move through this stage. Although some staff members would rather avoid the conflict of this stage, it is important to build skills and show them how to cope and deal with the storming stage.

Some staffs will remark, "We're in the storming stage. Something must be wrong." It is important to let your staff know that the storming stage is a naturally occurring stage of group development. Let them know that they are right on schedule. It just isn't necessary to spend the rest of the season in the storming stage. This is the perfect time to coach your staff so that they can progress beyond this stage. Some organizations will use DiSC, Myers-Briggs (MBTI), True Colors, and other inventories to analyze the work styles and behaviors of their staff. These instruments can be very helpful as staff members learn how to collaborate with each other, especially if they have different work styles.

The third, or *norming,* stage of group development is typically a welcome breath of fresh air after the storming stage. Although the staff is not yet at the highest performing stage, some of the bugs are now worked out within the group, and good things are beginning to happen. This stage of group formation includes cohesion, sharing and trust building, creativity, and skill acquisition. The director provides support during this stage and introduces the staff to tools and techniques that they can use to further improve their group development.

The *performing* stage is the fourth stage of group development and provides a feeling of unity, group identity, interdependence and independence. It is a stage of high productivity. Leadership from the director comes in the form of delegation. The staff has all the skills, resources and talent needed to complete the task. This stage can be explored using team challenge activities that require advanced skills, but which can be successfully accomplished by the group. Activities that build enthusiasm are also helpful here.

The *transforming* (or *adjourning*) stage is the final stage of group development. This stage allows your staff to conclude their time together, thanking each other and moving on at the completion of the project. This stage is marked by recognition by the director, conclusion, and disengagement by staff members. Feelings of celebration and affirmation are suitable. Different team members may experience this final stage at different rates. Don't rush for closure. For some staff members, this experience may have been one of the highlights of their life to date.

Now that all five stages of group development have been identified, here are some activities that you can use to explore each of these stages.

42. Believe It or Knot (Forming Stage)

This activity begins with small groups of five to six participants holding a knotted raccoon circle (either seated or standing). The knot is used as a pointer to identify the person talking. Begin by passing the knot to the right around the group. Someone says, "Stop!" and when the knot stops the person nearest to the knot is invited to disclose some interesting fact about themselves, such as, "I have a twin sister!" It is now the discussion and responsibility of the rest of the participants to decide whether they believe that this information is true or false. Group members can ask the person speaking a total of three questions. After some discussion, the group members give their opinion of the validity or falseness of the disclosure, and then the person providing the comment tells the truth.

After a person has revealed the true nature of their comments (true or false), they say "Left," or "Right," as they pass the knot around the group, and then "Stop!" as another member of the group has the opportunity to disclose something about themselves.

BOX 5.1 Believe It or Knot is similar to Two Truths and a Lie in that participants have the opportunity to evaluate the validity of another person's contribution. This is one activity that you can play anytime (or multiple times) with your staff. As the group develops, individuals are generally able to disclose information with increasing levels of intimacy. Two of the most interesting Believe It or Knot revelations (both of which were true) we've heard were, "My heart is on the opposite side!" And, "I had an 'arranged' marriage, and it is still working!"

43. Where Ya From? Where Ya Been? (Forming Stage)

Where Ya From? Where Ya Been? has become a great way for each member of a small group to share "their story." You'll need one knotted raccoon circle for each group of five to six participants. One at a time, each member of the group (with the help of all other group members) creates the outline perimeter shape of the city, town, county, state, or country of their birth, and then talks about life growing up in that location. This is the "where ya from" portion of the activity.

In a similar fashion, participants can choose to discuss "where ya been" information, and ask their small group to assist them in creating the perimeter shape of a place they have recently traveled. Be sure to encourage each person to discuss the significance of each location, in addition to forming the outline shape. For geographic locations, participants tend to form the outline of that location, but creative staff members can also create mountains, buildings, monuments, and other interesting destinations.

Encourage participants to create the shape of each location with other members of the group holding the Raccoon Circle, rather than placing it on the ground. By holding the Raccoon Circle, each member of the group is more actively connected to the group. When the Raccoon Circle is placed upon the ground, group members become spectators rather than participants in the activity. Small details like this make the difference between an actively engaged group and a potentially disengaged one.

Difficulties are just things to overcome, after all.
—Ernest Shackleton

BOX 5.2

At a youth leadership conference in Virginia, one keynote speaker mentioned that there are three unique things that each of us own: our name, our reputation, and our story. Where Ya From? Where Ya Been? is an activity that allows each person to tell their own story. Another unique feature about this activity is that the person speaking is often looking at the map, rather than at the other members of the group. For participants that are a bit hesitant to speak up in public, this format greatly reduces nervousness.

One of the unique connections made possible by this activity is when other members of the group have also been to the location discussed by any individual. A few years ago, two staff members from the same work group discovered that they had both grown up in the same state, in the same county, in the same town, and on the same street four houses apart, but at different times in their life. Activities that create this style of connection between the members of your staff will help reinforce the value and need for building positive relationships with other staff members.

Notes

■ 44. Cross the Line (Storming Stage)

This activity requires partners of equal body size to stand on opposite sides of a line. With half of the group about 3 feet (1 meter) behind one side of the line, and the other half of the team on the other side, the scene is set for a moment of conflict (of "us" versus "them") and to talk about win–win, win–lose, and lose–lose negotiation scenarios. You can use an unknotted Raccoon Circle, short piece of rope, masking tape, or even sidewalk chalk to create the line separating the two opponents.

Each side of the team says the following greeting to their opponents: "There ain't no flies on me, there ain't no flies on me, there might be flies on you (point to folks on the other side), but there ain't no flies on me!" Then the teammates boldly take a step toward the line (with just the right amount of attitude). The other side now repeats this greeting and takes a step toward the line. The first side now repeats, with twice the attitude, and moves to the line, followed by the second side repeating the lines and stepping face to face with the other side.

The facilitator now says, "You have three seconds to get the person across the line from you onto your side of the line. GO!"

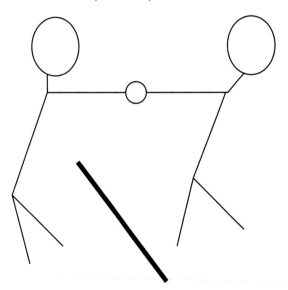

Typically, this phrasing results in a rather quick tug of war between partners, and usually a physical solution to the challenge. This provides an excellent opportunity to discuss conflict, challenges, attitude, negotiation, and how to resolve differences between people. For example, you can ask, "How many partner teams ended up in a win–lose scenario, where one member obtained what they wanted (getting their partner to their side), but the other member did not?" "What about a lose–lose scenario, where both members struggled, but neither one obtained the goal?" And finally, "Were there any teams that achieved a win–win solution, where both partners changed sides?" "What is it about our organization's culture that so many members of our team end up in win–lose or lose–lose scenarios, rather than a win–win solution?" "How can we fix this situation?" The next time you are in a cross-the-line situation, what is the first thing you will do to avoid a win–lose or lose–lose scenario?

Note: This activity does have a *strong physical component*. If you have staff members with mobility, balance, strength, or other body issues, you should suggest that they observe this activity, rather than participate.

You only ever grow as a human being if you're outside your comfort zone.
—Percy Cerutty

During one university residence hall staff-training program, this activity created some interesting and valuable comments from the members of the staff. It seemed that there was some serious *trash talking* happening in some areas of the residence halls, and that the behavior of students living in these areas was far from a win–win situation. The resident director of each hall utilized this activity with students to open the door to discuss what effect language was having on the attitudes, behavior, and culture of their living environment. When students realized that their language was contributing to the decay of their living society, they choose to modify their language and, in return, greatly improved their own environment.

Notes

The best way to escape from a problem is to solve it.
—Alan Saporta

▉ 45. People Movers (Storming Stage)

You can actually use this one activity to explore *all* the stages of group development: From the structure and order needed in the forming stage, through the conflict and chaos of the storming stage, into the cooperation and teamwork of the norming and performing stages, and finally, to the celebration and forward movement (on to another challenge) of the transforming (or adjourning) stage.

The example shown here utilizes an ideal group size of six members. Larger groups are possible, but not recommended. This activity is tough enough with six members. Eight or more, or an uneven number of members, make this activity more difficult than required. If you have more than six participants, try setting up several activity areas and let them run simultaneously.

Begin by placing seven sheets of paper on the floor or ground. For best results, use different color paper for each location, and place these seven pages in a smile-shaped arrangement, rather than the straight line shown here. This makes it easier for each member of the group to see all the other members of the group. Increased visibility enables increased communication.

Begin by asking each person to stand on one of the pieces of paper, facing toward the middle. The central, or middle, page is unoccupied at the start. The basic challenge of this activity is for the three members on the left side of the group to exchange places with the three members on the right side.

Although this activity has several standard rules that a facilitator can provide and that participants must following when changing locations, one of the most creative variations of this activity with your staff would be to allow them to work out, by trial-and-error, what these rules are. This concept of *learning the ropes,* or *failing forward,* as John Maxwell would phrase it, can create some interesting discussions at the completion of this challenge. Group members can move *any way* they choose, and get immediate feedback from the facilitator if that particular technique is allowable within the rules of the challenge. If a technique is not allowed, group members are encouraged to try again, but first to understand why a particular technique was not allowed.

Whether you plan to provide your group with instructions or allow group members to discover them on their own, here are the basic rules:

1. The goal is to have both groups of three change places.
2. Anyone *can* move into any open space directly in front of them.
3. Anyone *can* jump over (around) a member of the opposite group, into any open space.
4. You *cannot* pass a member of your own group.
5. You *cannot* back up.
6. Only one person can be actively moving at a time.
7. If you reach a position from which you cannot move forward, and the system becomes 'locked,' the entire group must return to the beginning and try again.

It takes a minimum of 15 moves to complete this challenge. Groups achieving success to this challenge can be further challenged by demonstrating that they can repeat their performance, but this time, without talking. As a final, high-level challenge, invite your group to complete this activity efficiently without breathing! That is, ask everyone in the group to simultaneously take a breath and hold it, start and complete the relocation, before anyone needs to breath again. Good luck!

For an interesting variation of this activity, try using chairs instead of sheets of paper to mark the location of each position.

 **BOX 5.5** Useful Hints: By placing all seven blocks (or sheets of paper) in a curved smile pattern instead of a straight line, all members of the group will be able to see each other, and communication and problem solving will be greatly enhanced.

Also, each time a group starts over, it is extremely helpful if they all return to their original starting position. Changing positions each round, while an interesting method of cross-training, can be confusing and generally increases the time required to successfully complete this challenge.

Notes

◼ 46. The Missing Link (Norming Stage)

This consensus-building activity requires two different colors of Raccoon Circles. One set of ropes is sufficient for up to 40 staff members to view. Begin by placing two Raccoon Circles on the floor. Tangle these two Raccoon Circles together, and tie both ends together (as shown in the illustration and photograph).

The basic goal of the missing link is for your entire staff to decide whether these two pieces of webbing are linked together (like links of a chain) or unlinked. If they are linked, then no amount of pulling will separate them. If they are unlinked, it will be possible to manipulate them so they are no longer touching each other.

Although visual puzzles like this are creatively fun ways to introduce problem solving techniques, there is another opportunity here. Invite members of your staff to choose a side. On the left side—staff members that believe these two ropes are linked. On the right side—those that think these two ropes are unlinked. Now that it is visually obvious where everyone stands, invite everyone to find a partner with the opposite choice. These two (or more) partners now have two minutes to come to consensus regarding their decision.

This style of listening to another person with a different opinion is critical for teamwork. By listening to your partner, you begin to understand how others approach the problem and how they go about solving it.

At the two-minute mark, invite partners to stay together and to choose a side. Chances are that you still will not have complete consensus, even by using the *pairing-and-sharing* technique. At this point, *slowly* begin to untangle the two Raccoon Circles, and allow members from either side to change sides if they wish. As the ropes become untangled, it become more and more clear whether they are linked or unlinked. By using this technique, even staff members who have chosen the incorrect side are allowed to learn from their mistake and are welcomed to the eventually correct side.

Although the actual solution may be simple or complex, the real value of this activity comes from a team working together to achieve a group consensus, listening to each other, and learning the skills that it takes to get everyone on the same page. The process known as *pairing and sharing* is very important and involves everyone working with a partner in an attempt to convince one other person before trying to convince the entire group. This technique is not only useful in problem-solving situations like The Missing Link, but can also be used with other work related problems and challenges.

After revealing the true nature of the tangled Raccoon Circles (linked or unlinked), discuss with the group their problem solving techniques. How many

people changed sides because of their partner's beliefs? For the side that was eventually correct, why didn't they manage to attract more people to their side? How many people were sure the moment they first saw the Raccoon Circles, which side was the right side? How many people changed sides several times, and still weren't sure?

47. Eagle in the Wind (Norming Stage)

After some initial trust-building activities (such as The Blind Trust Drive, found as activity #5 in this book), here is a wonderful higher-level trust activity. You'll need a flat open space, and at least 12 people. The facilitator demonstrates this activity by volunteering to be the first eagle. Other team members form the outer circle, standing about 6 feet (2 meters) apart from each other. The eagle closes their eyes, spreads their arms (like wings), and flies a straight path (jogs slowly) toward the outside members of the circle. As they approach the circle, one team member says, "I've got you," and grasps one of the eagle's wrists, twirling them around until they are again facing toward the center of the circle, and then letting go. The eagle continues their flight, to another person in the circle who again twirls them back into the circle, for a total of five or six flights.

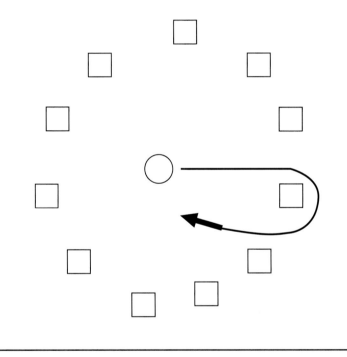

Thanks to Sam Sikes for allowing us to share this wonderful trust building activity. You can find more information about his work and his teambuilding books at: www.doingworks.com.

Notes

48. Grand Prix Racing (Performing Stage)

Knot a Raccoon Circle into a complete loop using a water knot and you are ready for the ultimate in sport racing. Thanks to Tom Heck, not only for the idea for this activity, but also for the enthusiasm to lead it effectively. This activity will boost the enthusiasm of your audience and provide some moderate competition in the process.

Begin by spreading several knotted Raccoon Circles around the available space, in close proximity to each other. Ask participants to join one of the "racing teams," picking their favorite color team in the process. Approximately six to eight participants per Raccoon Circle. Have participants hold the Raccoon Circle with both hands in front of them. Say the following:

Ladies and gentlemen! It is summertime, and that means one thing in this part of the world—Grand Prix Racing! Now I know that you are such die-hard race fans that just the thought of a race makes your heart beat faster. So this race comes in three parts. First, when I say, "We're going to have a race," your response is loud, "Yahoo!!" Next I'll say, "Start your engines!" and I want to hear your best race car sounds (audience practices making race car revving engine, shifting gears and braking sounds).

Finally, with so many cars on the track today, it will be difficult to see just which group finishes the race first, so we'll need a sign indicating when your group is finished. That sign is to raise your hands (and the Raccoon Circle) above your heads and yell, "Yesssssssss!"

Logistically, Grand Prix involves having the group transfer the knot around the group as quickly as possible, using only their hands. This activity can even be performed for a seated audience. To begin, you'll need a "start/finish" line, which can be the person that was born the farthest distance away from the present location. The race begins at this location and ends when the knot is passed around the circle, and returns to this same location (Yesssssssss!)

Typically in Raccoon Circle Grand Prix racing, there are three qualifying rounds or races. The first race is a single-lap race to the right, with the knot traveling once around the inside of the circle to the right (counterclockwise). The second race is a multilap race (two or three laps) to the left (clockwise) around the circle. And the final race of the series is a

"winner-take-all" championship race, with one lap to the right (counterclockwise), followed by one lap to the left (clockwise).

Incidentally, after this activity, the group will not only be energized, but perhaps in a slightly competitive mood. From a sequencing standpoint, you can either continue this atmosphere with more competitive challenges or introduce a bit of counterpoint, by following this activity with one that requires the group working together in a collaborative manner.

49. Sunny Side Up

Here is an activity that only requires a tarp (or shower curtain or large tablecloth) and a tennis ball, but will captivate your staff until they get it right! This activity can be used to reinforce the nine problem-solving steps introduced in the last chapter. Best of all, this is exactly the kind of activity that creates engagement of all team members and a satisfying cheer when the activity is successfully completed.

Begin with an inexpensive tarp, available in most hardware stores. You can choose almost any size, but a 6 foot × 8 foot (2 × 3 meters) tarp is perfect for a group of six to eight participants. If you have more than eight staff members, you'll need more than one tarp. You'll also need one tennis ball for each tarp.

The challenge of this activity is for the group to successfully launch the tennis ball upward from the middle of the tarp, and to turn over the tarp so that the ball lands on the opposite on the way back down. The motion of the group is then, toss the ball upward, flip over the tarp, catch the ball.

To further encourage your staff to plan their work, invite them to try working through possible techniques *without the ball*. Each team can actually practice as many times as they want without the ball. But with the ball (just like with a customer, client, or camper), they only have one chance to get it right!

You'll know when your staff accomplish this challenge. Most teams will cheer loudly when they actually are successful. Discussion topics for this activity include reviewing the problem-solving and planning process. You can also discuss what other staff responsibilities are like this challenge—you only have one chance to get them right!

50. A Circle of Kindness (Transforming Stage)

Here is an activity with just the right amount of ceremony that is perfect for bringing closure to the end of the season. In a very private and personal way, every member of the group is recognized, affirmed, and celebrated.

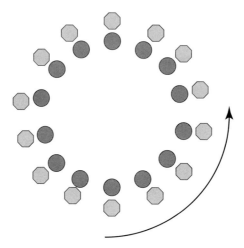

This activity begins with half of the group forming a circle, with everyone facing the center. The rest of the group forms a second circle (also facing the center of the circle) so that each member of the outer circle is standing just behind a member of the inner circle.

Invite the members of the inside circle to close their eyes. Outer circle members are invited to place their hands on the shoulders of the person directly in front of them. This spacing allows the members of the outside circle to whisper into the ear of the person in front of them.

Encourage members of the inner group that this is not a conversation, but rather, that they are on the receiving end of some very positive comments from their partners. The most they can respond is, "Thank you." This avoids breaking the mood with laughter, giggling or any other fun but disruptive conversation.

Outside circle members are encouraged to tell their partner something they value about them. Typical comments might include, "It was great working with you this summer," or, "I'm so glad we were on the same team this year."

When finished, the members of the outside circle move one person to their right, and the process continues until they have encountered all members of the inside circle. At this point, the members of both circles switch places, and the process continues.

Be sure to allow adequate time for this activity. If this is one of the last opportunities for your staff to be together, each interaction can take a minute or more. That means for a group of 40 staff members, you'll need 40 minutes to complete this activity (and then some).

If you'd like to complete the ceremonial atmosphere of this activity, you can include candles at the center of the group. Firelight also creates a warm atmosphere for this activity.

---

51. The Four-Minute Team (Transforming Stage)

Here is an interesting closing activity for any size group. It is best to start this activity with group members scattered randomly about the area (i.e., *not* in a circle).

Say, "Everyone knows that the ultimate test of teamwork is for a team to hold their arms outstretched (demonstrate, with arms stretched parallel to the ground) for four minutes. It is impossible for many groups, but I think a great team like this one can probably do it! Ready, begin!"

It can be extremely uncomfortable to hold you arms stretched outwards for four minutes. But, by placing your arms on the shoulders of other team members, the challenge becomes easier for everyone! A neat trick, and a great metaphor for teamwork from this closing activity.

Notes

◼ Conclusion

Here are a few final suggestions for helping your staff understand and navigate these five stages of group development.

Be sure to inform your staff that there are no value judgments related to each of these stages. That is, each stage is neither good nor bad. They are all normal and necessary in the development of a group. Some are obviously more stressful than others, but with the right tools, properly applied, all stages can be successfully navigated.

One of the classic mistakes made by group leaders is underestimating the influence that can occur in a group when new members join the group (or existing members leave). Even a high-performing group can slip back a few stages when the membership in a group changes. Be prepared. And be sure to allow time for new members to progress through the stages, just as you did with the entire group. In a similar way, the departure of various group members may not happen simultaneously. In this case, you'll need to create a suitable time to help the entire group adjourn or transform.

Do not expect that just because 90 percent of your staff have learned how to identify and navigate these stages of group development, that the other 10 percent joining a bit later will automatically be influenced by this prior process. The good news is that when a new member joins the group, you can invite members of your existing staff to take them through this process.

The stages of group development are based on the research of Bruce Tuckman. For more information about this work, review the following articles:

- "Developmental Sequence of Small Groups," Bruce Tuckman, 1965, *Psychological Bulletin*, Number 63, pages 384–399. The classic original paper.
- "Stages of Small Group Development Revisited," Bruce Tuckman and Mary Ann Jenson, 1977, *Group and Organizational Studies*, Number 2, pages 419–427. In this paper, the fifth stage (adjourning) was added.
- "Developmental Sequence in Small Groups," Bruce Tuckman, 2001, *Group Facilitation*, Number 3, Spring, pages 66–81. A look back, nearly 35 years after the original ground-breaking paper. This article should be required reading for all group facilitators. In this article, Tuckman himself mentions that most of the initial research and data collected on this subject was provided from therapy groups rather than natural work teams. In support of this comment, however, many natural work groups could use a bit of therapy occasionally!

The stages of group development model proposed by Tuckman is not the only model of group development. In her book *Theories of Small Group Development*, Dr. Raye Kass of Concordia University presents five different theories of small group development. One is likely to describe your staff! The fourth edition of this book, printed in 2008, is available from the Centre for Human Relations and Community Studies, Concordia University, Montreal, Quebec, ISBN 978-0-9810500-0-3.

Creative Presentation Techniques

6

As mentioned in the opening pages of this book, the activities presented here are intended to create a meaningful experience for your staff and open the door to conversations and discussions that will further enhance your staff-training program. The importance and value of the review and debriefing component in adventure-based and active learning is significant. Equally important is the front-loading or framing that begins each activity.

This chapter is provided to acquaint you with several valuable approaches to preparing, delivering, and debriefing the activities in this book. Consider this collection of tools a small sample of our favorite techniques. For even more processing, debriefing, reviewing and reflection activities and techniques, see the book *A Teachable Moment* by Jim Cain, Michelle Cummings, and Jennifer Stanchfield, from Kendall/Hunt Publishers, ISBN 0-7575-1782-X.

BOX 6.1

While walking one day, a man recognized me and explained that he had been in a group I had facilitated some years earlier. He introduced me to his walking partner. *"I told you about this guy, he's the one who taught amoebas to do circus tricks in a lab dish."* I was embarrassed to explain that the bit about teaching amoebas to jump through hoops was just a story I used to introduce the learning activity that followed. Now it was his turn to be embarrassed. We shared an awkward laugh and wished each other well. But then I asked him if he remembered the discussions that followed the story and activity. He thought about it for a moment and then said, *"No, I just remember your story."* At that point, I made a commitment to place less emphasis on storytelling and devote greater effort to creating more concrete connections between activities and the learning outcomes they were selected to achieve.

A true story, from Dave Knobbe

◼ Story-Based and Metaphor-Rich Briefings

Keeping activity briefings fresh and interesting without making the storyline overpowering is a delicate balancing act. Here are two techniques for briefing (or frontloading) an activity. To contrast these two approaches, both examples involve the popular activity *River Crossing*. A summary of this simple but powerful activity follows.

52. River Crossing

River Crossing is an excellent activity choice for helping groups define norms around problem solving. Follow-up discussions often center on the importance of planning and how members support each other's success. You'll need several objects to mark boundaries and 8 to 10 flat, lightweight objects to use as *stepping stones*. Carpet squares, placemats, paper plates or small boards are suitable stepping stones for this activity.

The *river* in this activity is the boundary defined by the cones in the illustration. The total distance should require a group to move each of their stepping stones at least once while crossing. The challenge of this activity is for the group to successfully cross the river, using the stepping stones, and reach the other side. There are (of course) a few guidelines for the safe and efficient use of the stepping stones. Only the stones can come in contact with the ground or floor (the river). Stones must be in contact with at least one member of the group at any time or they are immediately lost. While these metaphorical stones are lightweight, consider them real stones—so no throwing allowed.

Instead of establishing a *do or die, all or nothing* mentality to this activity, discuss with your group what a reasonable number of errors might be during the completion of this activity. Encourage the group to set a goal for themselves around these mistakes. Some failures (according to John Maxwell) can actually enable the group to move forward.

53. Story Cards

Story Cards are a creative technique for introducing an activity that places additional responsibility on the group to define the actual challenge.

Before the activity, create a series of (at most) 10 instruction cards. Present these cards in random order to the group at the beginning of the activity and let them decide what to do next. Examples of the content of these cards for the River Crossing activity are listed next.

Some intentional ambiguity in the instructions creates an interesting dynamic as the group struggles to define the task. When the group asks for clarity, unless the question revolves around issues of physical or emotional safety, the facilitator typically responds by saying, *"You have the information you need to be successful."* The group's *interpretation* of the instructions can often create imaginary boundaries and obstacles, delaying or even eliminating a successful completion of the activity. These will become valuable topics to consider in the post-activity reviewing process.

Ten Story-Based Briefing Cards—River Crossing

A river rages before you. What you seek is on the other side.

This river is far too swift to enter and impossible to walk around.

The current is so strong that anyone touching it is swiftly swept away.

Leave no one, and nothing, behind.

Amazonian Flatback Swallerfish are impervious to the rushing water, and they float!

Swallerfish do not like to travel backward, and don't appreciate being handled roughly.

One fish can support the weight of at least one person.

Maintain contact with your fish at all times! Lose contact for even a second and it is gone for good.

You do not have unlimited time.

There are consequences for errors.

Metaphor-Rich Briefing—River Crossing

Rather than supplying all the details of a story for your group, consider the basic elements of the activity (the river, the stepping stones, the people involved, the time limit, etc.) and include the group in creating meaning from this activity. Instead of inventing rivers and fish, anchor the activity using tangible things that have relevance to the group. Create a powerful enough metaphor, and the transference of the lessons from this activity back to the workplace will be outstanding. For example, "Where is the group now?" Another way of asking this same question is, "What does this riverbank signify? Where does the group want to be at the end of their current project? What does it need to get there? What mistakes could keep the group from being successful?"

By using real-life examples as part of the activity, participants are able to connect learning from an offsite staff-training event to future work-related events. Continue this technique by placing something at the far boundary (riverbank) that this group wants to achieve. For example, you can ask each member of the group to write a goal for this project on an index card, collect these cards, place them in a container, and locate this container on the far side of the river. Finally, for this activity especially, you'll need an appropriate metaphor for the river. It should represent something that is keeping this group from realizing its goal. Perhaps it is a limitation of financial resources, or behaviors that do not help the group move forward. It can also be several things at once. Write some of these obstacles on index cards, and place them in the river near the path the group will take. As they surpass each of these obstacles, you'll create opportunities for a meaningful debriefing session. You can also create metaphors for the stepping stones, the time limitation, and any other pertinent component to this activity.

When the group has created all the necessary metaphors for the activity, encourage the group to begin, use its resources, conquer its obstacles and achieve its goals.

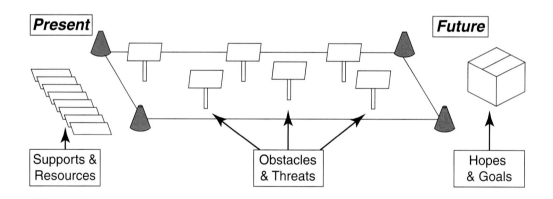

For a corporate teambuilding program with ten group members present, participants wrote down some individual goals and personal talents they had to share with fellow group members on their stepping stones. The river became a metaphor for reaching a better work environment from their present reality. With the group halfway across the river, I showed up on the original riverbank with another stepping stone. Metaphorically, I was the new employee that they were expecting to arrive (in reality) in the next week. I heard comments ranging from, *"I wouldn't want to be you,"* to *"just wait a few minutes, we'll come back for you when we finish what we're doing."* When the group eventually came back for me, and told me to drop my stepping stone in the water and join them, I did exactly that. I dropped the stepping stone I was holding . . . and the river's current (metaphorically) swept it away. *"I did what you said!"* I exclaimed. *"Did I do something wrong?"* After completing the activity, a serious discussion about how new employees are welcomed to the group occurred. This group even created a list of things-to-do for new employees. The metaphor worked for this group, and it became the richest debriefing session of the entire day.

Jim Cain

Good management is the art of making problems so interesting and their solutions so constructive that everyone wants to get to work and deal with them.
—Paul Hawken, *Growing a Business*

◼ Visual Profiles—An Effective Debriefing Technique

One shortcoming of group debriefings can occur when a member of the group offers the comment, *"I think we were thinking this. . . ."* or *"we were ready to move on."* Such global comments may be inaccurate for all members of the group. By using a more visual rather than verbal technique, it is possible to quickly gain a more accurate representation of the group's opinion on important issues.

Two techniques are introduced here. Team Performance cards and weather profiles both provide visual representations of group behaviors, beliefs, attitudes, and feelings. To maximize the utility of these cards, give each person a token of some kind, such as a small stone, coin, poker chip, or paper clip. Arrange a collection of visual profile cards in the center of the group. Pose a question to the group and instruct group members to place their token on the illustration that best represents their answer. Without any staff member saying a word, you'll instantly have an accurate representation of your group's opinion, graphically represented by the number of tokens on each portrait.

Illustrations of the Team Performance cards can be found in the Ready-to-Copy section of this book. Enlarge the size of these cards so that team members can easily see what is illustrated on each card.

One of the most interesting ways to create your own set of weather cards is to search for unique weather pattern illustrations on the Internet. Using Google, for example, click the *Images* button (in the upper-left-hand corner of the main Google search engine page). When you enter a word or phrase (such as *weather*), you'll receive hundreds of interesting weather photographs, illustrations, graphics, and images. Print these off to create weather patterns that are appropriate

metaphors for the groups you plan to facilitate. You'll find a page of weather cards in the Ready-to-Copy section of this book, and you can download these same weather cards in full size at the Essential Staff Training Activities page of the Teamwork & Teamplay Web site, at www.teamworkandteamplay.com.

Additional visual profile cards, such as the Chiji Cards produced by the Institute for Experiential Education in LaCrosse, Wisconsin (608) 784-0789, and the Organizational Images produced by RSVP Design Limited (www.rsvpdesign.co.uk), are also available from Training Wheels, Inc. (www.training-wheels.com).

Consider the distribution of X-shaped tokens on the group weather card profiles shown here. What might this profile suggest about what is currently happening within the group right now?

Be cautious when interpreting why other members of the group may have chosen a particular image or illustration. Let each person verbalize their own interpretation. One person might interpret a tornado as exciting and powerful, while someone else interprets the sun as symbolic of drought and hard times.

Here are three techniques for using visual assessment cards with your staff:

1. *Emotional check-in.* Assess how the group is feeling. Give each team member a token. Spread the weather profile cards in front of the group and ask each person to put a marker on the card that best reflects how they are feeling at that moment.
2. *Contribution continuum.* Conduct self-assessment and peer feedback. After an activity, place all the cards in a line. Ask individuals to assess their own performance and stand behind the card that best represents their contribution to the group's success. Invite everyone to explain their choices and allow others to challenge these assessments and assumptions.
3. *Highs and lows.* Retell my personal story. Spread the weather profile cards in front of the group and ask members to individually pick the two cards that represent what they experienced as the high and low points of their day. Invite everyone to explain their choices. Use this as an opportunity for feedback.

Notes

54. Team Performance Debrief Cards

The following cards illustrate several kinds of staff and team dynamics. Some illustrate high-performing groups. Others illustrate typical ways in which teams may fail to work together. You'll find 12 full-size versions of these cards in the Ready-to-Copy section of this book. Use these cards during staff training to encourage discussion about your staff's performance.

Here are three techniques for using team performance cards to help a group explore their dynamics as a team:

1. *Visual profiles.* Explore team dynamics. Give each staff member several tokens. Place all the team performance cards in front of the group and ask each member to place markers on the cards that best reflect their experience as part of the group. The result is a visual profile of the team's performance.

2. *Effectiveness continuum.* Set direction for improved performance. Ask the group to arrange the cards in order from the highest performing team to the team having the most problems. Then, ask the group where they believe they are along the continuum they have created. Next, ask the group where they would like to be along the continuum and explore what it would take for the team to reach this level. Use this as an opportunity to set several goals for improved team performance.

3. *Who am I? Who are you?* Reflect on roles and contributions. Place the team performance cards in front of the group. Ask individuals to identify the single character portrayed on the cards with whom they most strongly identify. Follow up by asking individuals to identify any characters that remind them of contributions made or roles played by other team members. Use this as an opportunity to encourage honest feedback between peers.

55. The Virtual Slideshow

One of the simplest and most powerful debriefing techniques is the Virtual Slideshow. Imagine that everyone in your group had a digital camera during today's program. At the final debriefing session, each person is asked to share some of their favorite images from the day. By pointing an imaginary slide projector "clicker" at an equally imaginary screen, staff members can *show* their images and narrate their favorite moments from the day. You can also use a genuine clicker available as a dog training device at most major pet stores.

In terms of the three traditional educational techniques (auditory, visual, and kinesthetic), this reviewing technique contains all three! The clicking sound (imaginary or real) is the auditory component. The visual content is supplied by the imaginary image. The act of physically pointing and clicking the device is the kinesthetic component. One technique—three teaching styles!

To further prepare your staff for this technique, and to allow adequate time for both fast-paced and slower-paced thinkers to create their images, invite everyone in the group to close their eyes. Instruct them to think of an image from today that was especially profound, or humorous, or inspiring. When each person has captured one image that fits this description, they can open their eyes. Now when the clicking device (imaginary or not) is passed to them, each person will be ready with a photograph already in their mind.

No use to shout at them to pay attention. If the situations, the materials, the problems before the child do not interest him, his attention will slip off to what does interest him, and no amount of exhortation of threats will bring it back.
—John Holt

◼ Multiple Intelligence Theory—A Framework for Engaging Youth More Effectively

This section, written by author Dave Knobbe, is directed primarily at organizations that serve youth as part of their mission. Although multiple intelligence theory is equally valuable to both youth and adult learners, the examples in this section will focus on engaging youth audiences.

Multiple intelligence (MI) learning theory is based on the concept that there is not a single universal intelligence but many different ones. Multiple intelligence theory provides an excellent foundation for engaging youth effectively. This section begins with a very brief overview of MI theory, followed by a sequence of activities that illustrates how our own behaviors as teachers, facilitators, trainers, and supervisors can profoundly impact our participation and outcomes for the youth we encounter.

We all have preferences for how we interact with our surroundings. These preferences color every choice we make when teaching, leading, or relating socially with others. Typically, we choose to operate in the mode that is most comfortable for us. Youth who "get" our style flourish in our groups, and we hold them up as examples of our own effectiveness. But what about children who don't interact with their surroundings in the same way the facilitator does? They tend to get bored and discouraged and check out.

How do we engage youth most effectively? First, we need to recognize their preferred way of interacting with their surroundings. Rather than lay responsibility on each child to pay attention to us teaching in the way that makes *us* feel most comfortable, we need to make it our job to find a way to reach each child by varying our approach. Each time you change the way you teach or the kinds of activities you offer, you allow different individuals to excel.

Step 1: Begin with Unstructured Playtime or a Brief Day-Dreaming Exercise

Give group members a few minutes to dream about how they would spend an unexpected day off where money wasn't any concern. How would they spend a whole day? Who would they spend it with? What would they do?

You might also consider providing a few playthings and a little unstructured time and afterwards asking people to consider how they used their time. Were they with others? By themselves? Did they write or draw or listen to nature sounds? How individuals answer questions like these provides a little insight into their preferred intelligences.

Step 2: Overview the Eight Intelligences

Verbal–Linguistic	Mastery of words and language, written and spoken
Interpersonal	Ability to connect with others and empathize with other's experiences
Intrapersonal	Clarity around internal feelings, commitment
Visual–Artistic	Mastery of shapes, diagrams, colors, maps, etc.

Mathematical–Logical	Ability to reason and solve problems based on logic and math
Body–Kinesthetic	Mastery of movement; interpretive dance, athletics, manipulation
Musical	Mastery of sounds and rhythms, including melodies and lyrics
Naturalist	Ability to understand natural processes and recognize differences in species, clouds, etc.

Each of us is a unique blend of all of these intelligences. We are not one or the other; however, one may be more dominant than the others.

At the time this book was in publication, a ninth intelligence was being considered: existentialism.

Step 3: Create a Visual Profile of Multiple Intelligences for Your Group

Have group members write their first name on three self-sticking note pages (two green and one red). Instruct participants to place their red note page on their least favorite multiple intelligence style and the two green notes on their favorite two styles. When complete, the visual profile will look something like this example:

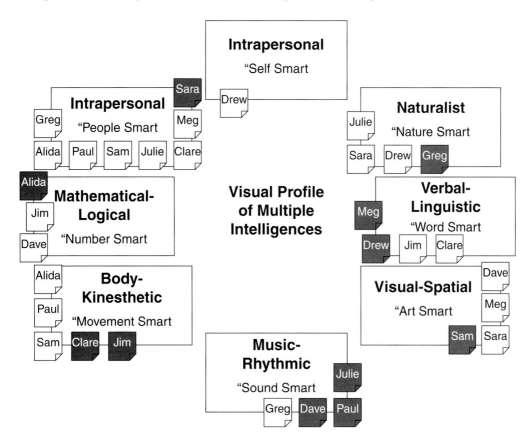

Step 4: Interpret the Group Profile

Look carefully at the groupings of greens and reds. These create a simple representation of the group. Talk about what the profile discloses about the group by asking questions like these:

- What does the profile suggest about the group's strengths and potential limits?
- Who are likely to be the best problem solvers?
- Who may be more excited about writing entries in a group journal?
- Who might be more attuned to an incoming storm?
- Who is likely to recognize when someone isn't feeling included?
- Which style is the preferred style for the greatest number of our group?

For the visual profile here, what would happen if Jim, Clare, Meg, and Drew—two of whom excel in verbal-linguistic intelligence and two of whom do not—are asked to write notes about the meeting?

Jim and Clare would most likely excel, while Drew and Meg would get bored and start doodling on their notepads or wander off in search of bugs.

Invite Drew to lead a nature hike or Meg to teach an art lesson, however, and both would happily and successfully rise to the challenge.

Other things this profile might suggest:

- This is a very social group
- Drew is the group's conscience (intrapersonal)
- Jim and Dave are problem solvers
- Sam, Paul, and Alida need to be kept physically busy
- Greg will lead if the task involves music

◼ Observing Multiple Intelligences in Action

For this series of activities, most group members are designated as *observers*. Their job is to watch multiple intelligence theory in action.

Lead four activities that explore different intelligences. For example, Arrowheads is a visual–spatial challenge, Tunes is a musical activity, Hieroglyphics is a verbal–linguistic challenge, and the Peteca is kinesthetic. Carefully choose a few individuals to demonstrate the activities who have either acknowledged that the targeted intelligence is their preferred mode or their least favored mode.

Observation Opportunity 1: A Visual–Spatial Challenge— Arrowheads

The Arrowhead challenge (activity #19 in this book) presents a visual-spatial conundrum. The task is to create a total of five arrowheads that are all the same size and shape as the one initially complete arrowhead, from the seven pieces provided. When complete, the group will be able to see all five arrowheads at the same time. For a more detailed description, see activity #19.

Observation Opportunity 2: A Musical–Rhythmic Challenge—Tunes

Using only metal spoons, a pitcher of water, and 8 to 10 drinking glasses, create a musical performance by playing a melody that the rest of the group will recognize. This activity is designated as activity #58 in this book.

Observation Opportunity 3: A Verbal–Linguistic Challenge—Hieroglyphics

Here is a linguistic challenge that you can share with your staff. The challenge is to decode each message. Begin this activity in groups of three. After a few minutes of problem solving, invite two groups to work together. You'll find a full-page version of hieroglyphics in the Ready-to-Copy section of this book and more detailed instructions with activity #38.

Hieroglyphics
Solve the following linguistic puzzles.

A.	UR	J.	_____ it	S.	(s)(s)(s)(s) (s)(s)(s) (s)(s) (s)
B.	Traveling CCCCCC	K.	TIMING TIM ING	T.	SOM
C.	2 UM + 2 UM	L.	bit MORE	U.	CY CY
D.	IDSK	M.	VAD ERS	V.	Going May 6 July 9
E.	HIJKLMNO	N.	O E O	W.	BAN ANA
F.	YOU/JUST/ME	O.	BJAOCKX	X.	ME QUIT
G.	LAL	P.	• THAT'S	Y.	SIGHT LOVE SIGHT SIGHT
H.	Often, Often, Often, Not, Not	Q.	nafish nafish	Z.	Wheather
I.	T I M E abdefgh	R.	more more more more more more more more		

Observation Opportunity 4: A Bodily–Kinesthetic Challenge—Peteca

A Peteca is a hand version of hackysack, similar to the shuttlecock used in badminton, but hit with the hands instead of a racket or paddle. The challenge of this activity is to keep the Peteca in the air for a total of 21 hits, without letting it touch the ground. You'll find fun variations described in activity #22 of this book.

Multiple intelligences provide a foundation for discussing differences in a positive, nonthreatening way. It makes it easy to focus on the value each person brings to the group and illustrates how diversity can be a component of team strength.

For more information about multiple-intelligence learning styles, read *Multiple Intelligences in the Classroom,* by Thomas Armstrong, ASCD Alexandria, Virginia, ISBN 0-87120-376-6.

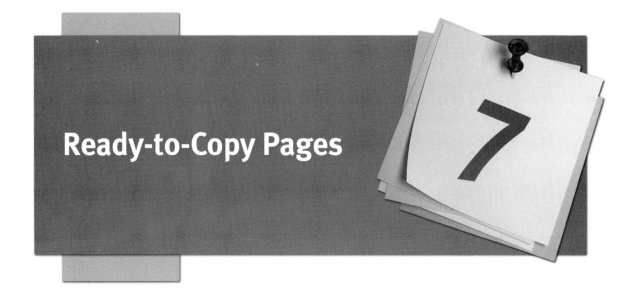

Ready-to-Copy Pages

This section contains complete, ready-to-copy versions of the following activities. Additional information about each of these activities can be found in Chapters 2, 3, and 4 of this book.

No.	Activity Name	Theme or Teachable Moment
2.	First Impressions	Get acquainted, avoiding stereotypes
8.	Character Cards	Character and team behavior
14.	Autographs	Icebreaker, task-growth-relationships
15.	The Big Question	Icebreaker, conversation
16.	The Big Answer	Icebreaker, giving advice
18.	Pieces of a Puzzle	Group problem-solving style
19.	Arrowhead Puzzle Profile	Synergy and teamwork
24.	Problem Solving Process Cards	Nine steps to problem solving
25.	The PVC Network	Problem solving and teamwork
38.	Hieroglyphics	Linguistic problem solving and groupwork
41.	10 × 10 × 10 Script	Leadership and teamwork
53.	How's the Weather Cards	Visual group assessment
54.	Team Performance Cards	Visual team performance behaviors

Copyright Permission

Purchasers of this book have the authors' permission to copy the pages in this section and use them with your staff training and teambuilding programs. All we ask is that the title of this publication and the authors' names appear at the bottom of each page.

Copyright permission does not extend to publications for sale, electronic databases, online Web site content, or other forms of electronic media. For permission for these types of information storage and usage, contact the authors directly.

First Impressions

Form a group of three, preferably with two other participants that you do not know very well (yet), and have a seat. Within this group, you are to guess the following traits about your partners. This is not a conversation; just make your best guess and write your answer in the outer spaces. When each of the three participants in your group has finished, begin sharing both your guesses and then the true information about each trait with each other. How many answers did you guess correctly?

	Person on your left side			Person on your right side	
Your Guess	The True Info	Traits	The True Info	Your Guess
		Where were they raised? (farm, city, suburbs, etc.		
		What type of student were they? (straight A's, honor roll, avg, etc.)		
		Their favorite food?		
		What type of music do they listen to? (rock, country, folk, hiphop, etc.)		
		What would their ideal job be?		
		What do you have in common?		

Character Cards

On the following pages, you'll find 12 different cards with character themes. Copy each of the cards twice for each set of character cards you wish to create. You can enlarge each illustration to fill one half of a regular sheet of paper. Use heavy copy paper or card stock and a color other than white to prevent the image from being seen through the opposite side.

For a large-format double-deck of character cards printed in full color (including character quotations), contact Creative Concepts at: www.GivaGeta.com or (860) 657-0770. With this deck of 58 cards, you can facilitate 11 different icebreakers, teambuilding challenges, and character-building activities, plus play all your favorite card games. Instructions are included.

You can also purchase these cards from Training Wheels, Inc. at 1-888-553-0147 or www.training-wheels.com.

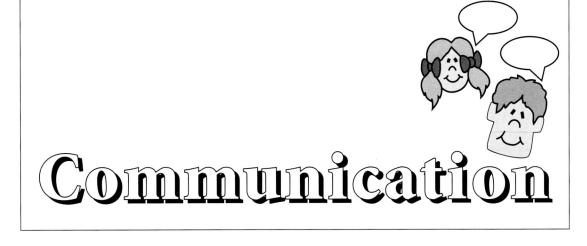

Communication

Teamwork

Respect

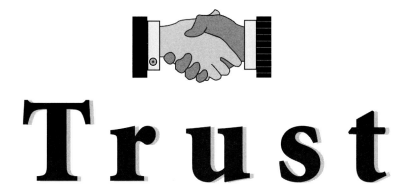

Trust

Helpfulness

Responsibility

Character

Appreciating
Diversity

LEADERSHIP

Positive Attitude

Honesty

CREATIVITY

Autographs

First, write your first name in the block below. Then find another person who **has done** (sign the top portion of the block) or **has not done** (sign the bottom portion of the block) any of the activities listed below. You can sign *up to two blocks* on anyone's autograph page.

Hello, my name is:

Your first name here, in great big letters.

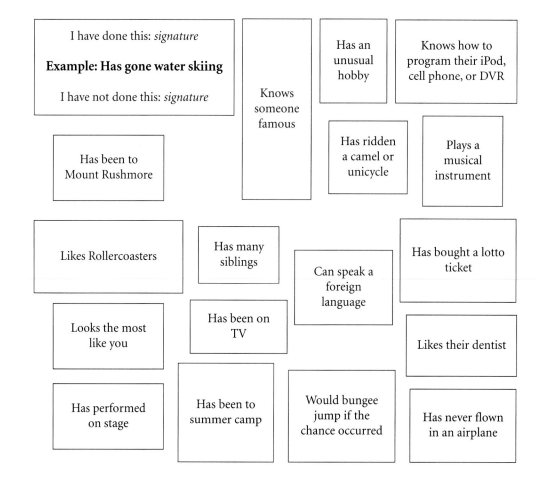

I have done this: *signature*

Example: Has gone water skiing

I have not done this: *signature*

Knows someone famous

Has an unusual hobby

Knows how to program their iPod, cell phone, or DVR

Has been to Mount Rushmore

Has ridden a camel or unicycle

Plays a musical instrument

Likes Rollercoasters

Has many siblings

Can speak a foreign language

Has bought a lotto ticket

Looks the most like you

Has been on TV

Likes their dentist

Has performed on stage

Has been to summer camp

Would bungee jump if the chance occurred

Has never flown in an airplane

The Big Question

At the bottom of this paper, write a question that you could ask to fellow participants if you were to interview them for a local radio talk show. For example, you might ask questions such as:

1. **What was the most unusual job you have ever had?**
2. **What is the definition of a life well lived?**
3. **Who has been the most influential person in your life, and why?**

You get the idea. Keep it clean, and be creative.

When you have finished writing your question, take this paper to the center of the room, find a partner, ask them your question, (they will answer it—you do not need to write the answer down) and then they will ask you their question (you answer it). When you are both finished talking, trade papers with this person. Then find a *new* partner—and ask them your *new* question,

Write your question here:

The Big Answer

We all have questions, for which we are constantly looking for answers. Write your choice of question in the space below. Let's see if we can help you generate some appropriate answers, or at least some food for thought.

My question is:

For those of you receiving this page, your task is to carefully consider the question above and write your best advice, answer, or comment in one of the spaces below.

Pieces of a Puzzle
for Staff Training

Instructions: Cut the following 12 clues into strips and pass out several to each member of the group. Answers for this activity can be found in Chapter 3 of *Essential Staff Training Activities*.

You may read this information out loud, but no one else may look at this paper.
Each staff visited the same four training locations, but in a different order.

You may read this information out loud, but no one else may look at this paper.
The first place the Australian group visited was Texas.

You may read this information out loud, but no one else may look at this paper.
Wyoming was the third training location the Australian group visited.

You may read this information out loud, but no one else may look at this paper.
In what order did the Italian group visit the training locations?

You may read this information out loud, but no one else may look at this paper.
The group that bought cell phones started their tour in Boston.

You may read this information out loud, but no one else may look at this paper.
Some information is irrelevant and will not help solve the problem.

You may read this information out loud, but no one else may look at this paper.
The English group visited Boston before Texas. The Italian group bought iPods in Wyoming.

You may read this information out loud, but no one else may look at this paper.
The Italian group visited New York after Boston. The Australian group received CPR training in Wyoming.

You may read this information out loud, but no one else may look at this paper.
Each staff visited their favorite training location last.

You may read this information out loud, but no one else may look at this paper.
The ACA took four staffs from four different countries on a tour of four training locations.

You may read this information out loud, but no one else may look at this paper.
Of the different staffs, the Dutch group liked Texas best.

You may read this information out loud, but no one else may look at this paper.
The Dutch group bought cell phones on their tour.

Arrowheads

You can use this illustration to make a pattern for your own arrowhead puzzle challenge. We suggest you make four complete arrowheads, and cut three of these into two separate pieces each (see photo).

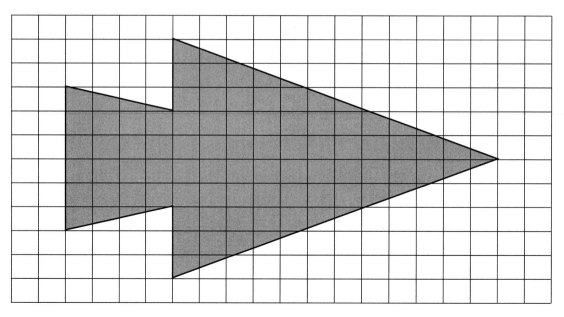

Problem Solving Cards

Nine Steps to Successful Problem Solving

Here and on the following pages you'll find the nine problem-solving process cards described in Chapter 3 of this book. Copy each of the following illustrations to create your own problem-solving process card deck. You can enlarge each illustration as necessary for your staff. Use a heavy copy paper and laminate your cards to preserve their appearance.

Define the Problem
Be sure everyone in the group clearly understands the problem or task, its parameters (rules), and goals.

Decide If the Problem Is Important
Decide if the problem or task is important enough to solve or carry out, and if the group has enough energy to solve the problem or complete the task.

Gather Information
The group gathers information by observation, asking questions, and physical contact with the resources.

Generate Ideas
Begin to collect all the ideas that the group can generate that might be part of solving the problem or completing the task. Avoid judging any ideas. Encourage combining ideas.

Develop a Plan
Identify the best ideas and combine ideas. Decide who needs to do what and when.

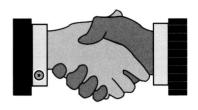

Communicate for Consensus
Be sure that everyone in the group fully understands the plan and agrees to make their best effort to help the plan succeed.

Do It!
Carry out the plan.

Evaluate the Outcome
Once the group carries out the plan, you must decide if you have the desired outcome.

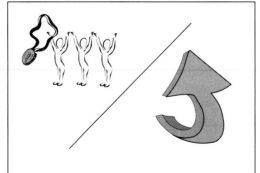

Celebrate Success or Return to First Step to Try Again.

The PVC Network

Project Description

Your group has been asked to build a complete "network" using *all* of the PVC tubes and connectors provided. Just like a water network, this collection of pipes and connectors must have no leaks. This means that each tube will have a connector at each end and that each connector will have a tube in each opening. The entire network will be interconnected. Your network design is a stand-alone architecture, so for this activity you are asked not to collaborate with other groups (they are attempting to solve the same problem with exactly the same pieces).

Here you will find several best-practice ideas for successfully completing this assignment. You can attempt to build your network without them, or use them from the very beginning. It's your choice.

When you are finished, ask several members of your group to read the self-evaluation questions on the next page and answer them as a group.

Best Practice Suggestions

1. Some connectors are more important than others. Which connectors should you use first? Why? Which connector should you use last? Attempt to use the connectors in descending order based on the number of holes in each one. Start with the four-way cross, then the T connectors, then the two-hole connectors (elbows and unions), and finish with the cap.
2. You'll probably need some long and short pipes throughout your construction efforts. So use some long and short pipes in the beginning and you'll have both styles left at the end. If you use *all* of the long or short pipes in the beginning, you won't have any of that style left to complete the project.
3. You should not have to force the pipes to make the network come together. If you have to forcefully bend and twist the structure to make connections—the system is trying to tell you something! Also, if the system keeps falling apart—it is trying to tell you that it doesn't want to be assembled that way. Try another strategy to find a more secure connection pattern.

Self-Evaluation Questions

1. What role did each member of the team perform? Who was the leader? The organizer? The project coordinator? The creative genius? The problem solver? The cheerleader? What other roles were apparent during the completion of this task?

2. How much time was spent planning the project before actual construction began? In the future, would you recommend more or less of this planning time?

3. Which of the following styles of problem solving were used by your group (circle one):

   1. trial and error   2. analyze, plan, perform   3. a really good guess and a whole lot of luck

4. After your group decided on a plan, did the group change the plan during the activity? If so, why?

5. How many ideas were considered during the early stages of the activity? Was each idea and each person given an opportunity to be heard?

6. Describe how each member of the group was given an opportunity to contribute to the group's success.

7. How would you rate your group's overall completion of this task?

8. In general, were the participants in your group more concerned about completing the task, or in caring for the members of the group? On the "football field of leadership" below, mark where your team was focused.

**Completing the
Task Endzone** 10   20   30   40   50   40   30   20   10 **Care for the Members
of the Group Endzone**

9. If you had the opportunity to perform this task again, what would you do differently?

10. If you were asked to give advice to a new team trying to accomplish this assignment, what information would you provide to help them be successful?

11. If you were going to hire an employee to complete this task, what skills would you want them to possess?

12. If you were chosen to lead the next group in successfully completing this activity, what style of leadership would you employ?

13. What were some of the best things you learned during this activity?

Hieroglyphics

Solve the following linguistic puzzles.

A.   UR

B.   Traveling
     CCCCCC

C.   2 UM + 2 UM

D.   IDSK

E.   HIJKLMNO

F.   YOU/JUST/ME

G.   LAL

H.   Often, Often, Often,
     Not, Not

I.   T   I   M   E
         abdefgh

J.   _____ it

K.   TIMING   TIM ING

L.   bit MORE

M.   VAD ERS

N.   [car with E]

O.   BJAOCKX

P.   • THAT'S

Q.   nafish   nafish

R.   more more more
     more   more
     more more more

S.   [S S S S / S S S / S S / S]

T.   SOM

U.   CY CY

V.   Going
     May 6 July 9

W.   BAN ANA

X.   ME QUIT

Y.   SIGHT   LOVE
     SIGHT
     SIGHT

Z.   Wheather

10 × 10 × 10: A Leadership Challenge Activity

Created by Dr. Jim Cain

The following script may be verbally shared with the group or given to the group leaders so that they can provide their group with this information.

Script

A simple definition of the project, for the leader:

Your assignment is to lead 10 people to move 10 feet in 10 minutes, using the 11 wooden walking boards provided. Begin by inviting your team members to stand on the wooden boards that have been placed in a U-shaped starting pattern. Each person begins by standing on two boards (one foot on each board).

Read the following information to your team:

My task is to lead this group, so that these 10 people move the 10 feet between these two lines in the next 10 minutes. The space behind the starting line is the practice zone. Any mistakes made in this region do not have any consequences. You are invited, and in fact encouraged, to experiment in this space. Here are a few rules:

- *Each rope may be held by only one person at any time.*
- *Only boards are allowed to touch the ground in the space between the two lines.*
- *During this activity, participants can touch only the boards on which they initially cross the starting line.*
- *Planning time is part of the 10-minute limit. The time clock begins now!*

How's the Weather?
Debriefing Cards

Use weather cards to quickly obtain an accurate profile of your group's attitudes, feelings, and beliefs about critical issues. See Chapter 6 for additional activity suggestions with these cards.

Team Performance Cards

See Chapter 6 for activity suggestions with these cards.

References and Resources

Here are a collection of valuable and useful references and resources for improving your staff training sessions.

Books and Articles

A Teachable Moment—A Facilitator's Guide to Activities for Processing, Debriefing, Reviewing & Reflection, 2005, Jim Cain, Michelle Cummings & Jennifer Stanchfield, Kendall/Hunt Publishers, Dubuque, IA USA www.kendallhunt.com (1-800-228-0810), ISBN 0-7575-1782-X. Adventure-based and active learning activities open the door for meaningful conversations about subjects that matter. Learn how to go beyond just the activities with these tools.

Active, Involved and Interested—Five Tips for More Meaningful Training, Beth Morrow, *Camp Business Magazine* (September/October 2008), pp. 28–29. Five simple techniques to improve your staff-training sessions.

Audio-Visual Methods in Teaching, revised edition, Edgar Dale, 1954, Dryden Press, ASIN B000K7P19S Edgar Dale is the originator of the *cone of learning.*

Brain Gym, revised teacher's edition, 1989, Paul and Gail Dennison, Edu-Kinesthetics, Inc., Ventura, California, USA ISBN 0-942143-02-7. This book covers all the brain gym basic movements.

Brain Gym and Me: Reclaiming the Pleasure of Learning, 2006, Paul Dennison, Edu-Kinesthetics, Inc. ISBN 978-0942-143-11-9.

Developmental Sequence of Small Groups, Bruce Tuckman, *Psychological Bulletin,* 63 (1965), pp. 384–399. The classic original paper from the researcher who coined the terms *forming, storming, norming,* and *performing.*

Developmental Sequence in Small Groups, Bruce Tuckman, *Group Facilitation,* 3 (Spring 2001), pp. 66–81. A look back 35 years after the original groundbreaking paper. Required reading for all group facilitators. In this article, Tuckman himself mentions that most of the initial research and data collected on this subject was provided from therapy groups rather than natural work teams. In support of this comment however, many natural work groups could genuinely benefit from therapeutic techniques!

Educating for Character—How Our Schools Can Teach Respect and Responsibility, 1991, Thomas Lickona, Bantam Books, New York, NY USA ISBN 0-553-37052-9. Teaching character and more.

Experiential Learning: Experience as the Source of Learning and Development, David Kolb, 1983, FT Press, ISBN 978-0132952613.

Flow—The Psychology of Optimal Experience, Mihaly Csikszentmihalyi, 1990, Harper Perennial, New York, NY USA ISBN 0-06-092043-2.

In Their Own Way, 2000, Thomas Armstrong, Jeremy Tarcher/Putnam, New York, NY USA ISBN 1-58542-051-4. Discovering and encouraging your child's multiple intelligences.

Learning Leadership, Michael Brandwein, 2003, YMCA of the USA, Chicago, IL USA ISBN 0-7360-5147-3. How to develop outstanding teen leadership training programs at camp.

Learning—Nineteen Scenarios from Everyday Life, Gerhard Steiner, 1999, Cambridge University Press, Cambridge, UK, ISBN 0-521-47800-6. A view of learning from many different perspectives, in everyday situations.

Making Ideas Stick—Why Some Ideas Survive and Others Die, 2007, Chip and Dan Heath, Random House, New York, NY USA ISBN 978-1-4000-6428-1. These authors introduce the SUCCESS model for creating an interesting learning environment.

Multiple Intelligences in the Classroom, 2000, Thomas Armstrong, ASCD Alexandria, Virginia USA ISBN 0-87120-376-6. This is an excellent template for designing your own curriculum with multiple possibilities for reviewing and learning in different ways.

Multiple Intelligences—The Theory in Practice, 1993, Howard Gardner, BasicBooks, New York, NY USA ISBN 0-465-01822-X. A fairly pedagogical presentation of multiple intelligences from the originator.

Practices That Support Teacher Development, Ann Lieberman, *Phi Delta Kappan,* 76, no. 8, pp. 591–596. "What everyone appears to want for students—a wide array of learning opportunities that engage students in experiencing, creating and solving real problems, using their own experiences and working with others—is for some reason denied to teachers when they are learners." "People learn best through active involvement and through thinking about and becoming articulate about what they have learned."

Research-Based Strategies to Ignite Student Learning: Insights from a Neurologist and Classroom Teacher, 2006, Judy Willis (ISBN 978-1416603702).

Shouting Won't Grow Dendrites: 20 Techniques for Managing a Brain-Compatible Classroom, 2006, Marcia L. Tate, Corwin Press, Thousand Oaks, CA USA ISBN 978-1412927802.

"Sit and Get" Won't Grow Dendrites: 20 Professional Learning Strategies That Engage the Adult Brain, 2004, Marcia L. Tate, Corwin Press, Thousand Oaks, CA USA ISBN 978-0761931539. Brain research focused on the adult learner.

Smart Moves—Why Learning Is Not All in Your Head, 1995, Carla Hannaford, Great Oceans Publishers, Arlington, VA USA ISBN 0-915556-27-8.

Social Intelligence, Daniel Goleman, 2006, Bantam Dell, New York, NY USA ISBN 978-0-553-80352-5. The new science of human relationships.

Stages of Small Group Development Revisited, Bruce Tuckman and Mary Ann Jenson, 1977, *Group and Organizational Studies,* Number 2, pages 419–427. This second paper added the fifth stage of group development known as *adjourning.*

Super Staff SuperVision, Michael Brandwein, 2002, Lincolnshire, IL USA ISBN 0-9670321-1-3. A how-to handbook of powerful techniques to lead camp staff to be their best.

Teambuilding Puzzles—100 Puzzles for Creating Teachable Moments in Problem Solving, Group Decision Making, Consensus Building, Goal Setting & Teamwork, 2005, Mike Anderson, Jim Cain, Chris Cavert and Tom Heck, ISBN 0-9746442-0-X. Engaging activities that you can use to reinforce essential life skills, corporate skills, and core values. 304 pages. Available from Training Wheels, Inc. at 1-888-553-0147 or *www.training-wheels.com.*

Teamwork & Teamplay, 1998, Jim Cain and Barry Jolliff, Kendall/Hunt Publishers, Dubuque, IA USA www.kendallhunt.com (1-800-228-0810), ISBN 0-7872-4532-1. "A Guide to Challenge and Adventure Activities that Build Cooperation, Teamwork, Creativity, Trust, Communication and Creative Problem Solving Skills." 417 pages of award-winning teambuilding knowledge and expertise.

Telling Ain't Training, Harold Stolovitch and Erica Keeps, 2002, ASTD Press, Alexandria, VA USA ISBN 978-1562863289. In addition to fascinating information about training, this book also has an extensive bibliography of additional references.

The Empty Bag—Non-Stop, No-Prop Adventure-Based Activities for Community Building, 2003, Chris Cavert and Dick Hammond, FUNdoing Publications, www.fundoing.com. ISBN 0-9746442-1-8.

The Revised and Expanded Book of Raccoon Circles, 2007, Jim Cain and Tom Smith, Kendall/Hunt Publishers, Dubuque, IA USA, www.kendallhunt.com (1-800-228-0810), ISBN 0-7575-3265-9. "More than two hundred simple activities that explore community building, social capital, and creative problem solving, using just a piece of tubular webbing.

The Summer Camp Handbook, 2000, Chris Thurber and Jon Malinowski, Perspective Publishing, Los Angeles, CA USA ISBN 1-930085-00-1. Everything you need to find, choose, and get ready for overnight camp—and skip the homesickness.

Training Terrific Staff!, Michael Brandwein, 2004, Lincolnshire, IL USA ISBN 0-9670321-2-1. A handbook of practical and creative tools for camp.

Training Terrific Staff! Volume Two, Michael Brandwein, 2008, Lincolnshire, IL USA ISBN 0-9670321-3-9. More great tools for outstanding staff development.

Worksheets Don't Grow Dendrites: 20 Instructional Strategies That Engage the Brain, Marcia L. Tate, 2003, Corwin Press, Thousand Oaks, CA USA ISBN 0-7619-3881-8.

✚ Web Sites

www.funderstanding.com	Whole-brain teaching techniques
www.jigsaw.org	The jigsaw classroom, a cooperative learning technique
www.ntlf.com/html/lib/bib/91-9dig.htm	Active learning excitement in the classroom
www.ncsu.edu/felder-public	Active and cooperative learning
www.braingym.org	Brain Gym information
www.C5yf.org	Web site of the C5 Youth Foundation
www.aca-camps.org	The American Camp Association official Web site; includes research and education pages
www.michaelbrandwein.com	Michael Brandwein's Web site
www.campspirit.com	Chris Thurber's Camp Leadership Essentials Web site
www.elearning.campspirit.com	1-877-237-3931
www.reviewing.co.uk	Roger Greenaway's excellent reviewing Web site
www.teachmeteamwork.com	Tom Heck's valuable teambuilding activity Web site
www.training-wheels.com	Michelle Cummings' Web site, where you can order most of the equipment used in this book
www.teamworkandteamplay.com	Author Jim Cain's teambuilding Web site. In addition to some great teambuilding ideas, this site also has a collection of free, downloadable instructions for activities and playful equipment that you can make yourself, including: Peteca (featherball) games, Horseshoe Golf instructions, Using Dance to Create Community, a collection of Raccoon Circle activities, songs, games, and staff training ideas.

A Note of Thanks

Our professional careers as facilitators, trainers, teachers, and authors have brought us in contact with many talented people who have generously shared their talents and wonderful ideas with us over the years. We are also grateful for the opportunity to train and work with so many energetic staff members from around the world, who have also given us great ideas for improving the quality of staff-training programs. On behalf of all of us (Jim, Clare-Marie, and Dave), thank you for your friendship, for your great ideas, and for allowing us to share these ideas with the world.

We would like to especially thank the following: Chris Cavert, Dick Hammond, Michelle Cummings, The Wyman Center, Tom Heck, Mike Anderson, Faith Evans, Camp Fiver, Cornell University Outdoor Education (COE), Tom Smith, Deb Jackson, Mary Kausch, Dave Moriah, Albuquerque YMCA, Sam Sikes, Allison Williams, Claire Wyneken, Bill Henderson, Kirk Weisler, Allison Phaneuf, Bob Faw, Tim Borton, Jennifer Stanchfield, Barry Jolliff, Camp Stone, YMCA Mission Valley, Kate and Jeff North, Betsy Jeff Penn 4-H Center, John Schultz, Thomas Armstrong, Carla Hannaford, Marcia Tate, Paul Dennison, Jeff Cohen, Allyson Burley, Deb Donohoe, Robert Watson, Charles Williams, Gabe Campbell, Mike Currence, David Kolb, Michael Brandwein, Chris Thurber, Chip and Dan Heath, Tom Andrews, Robert Fulghum, Tom Rath, Byrdie Baylor, and Joanna Carolan.

About the Authors

Dr. Jim Cain is the author of the teambuilding texts *Teamwork & Teamplay; The Revised and Expanded Book of Raccoon Circles; Teambuilding Puzzles; A Teachable Moment;* and this book, *Essential Staff Training Activities.* He is a former executive director of the Association for Challenge Course Technology, a senior consultant to the Cornell University Corporate Teambuilding Program, and the founder, director, and creative force behind his training company, Teamwork & Teamplay. Dr. Cain frequently serves as a staff development specialist on building unity, community, connection, leadership, engagement, and teamwork. He has shared his knowledge with individuals and organizations in 46 states and 17 countries (so far).

Jim Cain
Teamwork & Teamplay
468 Salmon Creek Road
Brockport, NY 14420 USA

Phone (585) 637-0328

jimcain@teamworkandteamplay.com

www.teamworkandteamplay.com

Building Unity, Community, Connection, Leadership, Engagement,
and Teamwork through Active Learning.

Clare-Marie Hannon is the director of Support Services for the Association of C5 Youth Foundations with partner organizations in Atlanta, Los Angeles, Boston, and Austin. She began her career coordinating the camping programs for the Florida Department of 4-H and Youth Development and then dedicated 13 years of her life as an educational center and camp director and as a youth development specialist with the Department of 4-H Youth Development in North Carolina. She has served as the director of Professional Development for The Wyman Center of St. Louis and the Camp Coca-Cola Foundation, and is a frequent trainer, speaker, and organizational development facilitator for not-for-profit organizations, teachers, camp staffs, and youth development professionals. Clare-Marie is a prolific writer of training and youth development curricula. Early in her career, she designed curriculum and training tools for use in Thai villages and trained community educators in Thailand.

Clare-Marie is the founder and executive director of TLC (Teaching in a Living Classroom) Training Resources. Her company's mission is to bring innovative approaches to training and education, and to remind us that *learning is life's greatest adventure!* She is also the proud mother of Meghan Mauria Hannon, her training assistant, shown here preparing a PVC teambuilding activity.

Clare-Marie Hannon
TLC Training Resources
321 Bouldercrest Way
Woodstock, GA 30188 USA

Phone (678) 492-4394

claremarie-h@earthlink.net

Interestingly enough, **Dave Knobbe** never intended a career in outdoor education or youth development. While working on his master's degree in psychology at the University of Missouri, Dave took what was supposed to be a short break to try his hand at directing summer camp with the Wyman Center of St. Louis. Fifteen years later, after a string of position changes with increasing responsibility (which kept things interesting and provided lots of room for creativity), Dave joined the national team of the Camp Coca-Cola Foundation in Atlanta as director of Program Development and Best Practices.

He played a significant role in developing and updating Camp Coca-Cola's five-year leadership curriculum for teens, writing lesson plans, sequencing activities, and coaching seasonal and professional staff to deliver quality experiences for more than 1,200 youth-enrolled nationally. Dave considers his role as chief designer of the *Paintrock Leadership Challenge,* an intensive two-week experience in remote Wyoming that helps youth anchor visions of career and college success in a powerful "journey" metaphor, among his proudest professional accomplishments. This experience has become a centerpiece of the five-year curriculum.

In 2007, Camp Coca-Cola became the C5 Youth Foundation. A year later, Dave became the executive director of the C5 Youth Foundation's Texas program.

Dave and his wife, Julie, were blessed with twins in 2001, and with a son just two years later. Dave and Julie delight in their children's exploits as gardeners, dancers, artists, big game hunters (lizards, actually), and readers.

In 2004, Dave earned a bachelor's degree in counseling psychology from the University of Missouri, Columbia. Finishing his master's degree still ranks high on his *"50 things to do before I'm done"* list.

Dave Knobbe
1491 Oak Springs Drive
Marietta, GA 30062 USA

Phone (770) 509-8528
Phone (770) 712-8524

kodah4@msn.com

Inspiration

Written on the western beach of Paget Island, Bermuda

If you are wondering where the inspiration to write this book originated, there are three sources.

First, in July, after a busy training season in the United States, I flew to Europe to work with several organizations there. Having just completed more than 30 summer-camp staff-training programs, I had recent data on which activities were both well received and valuable to the audiences I'd served in the past two months. Several camp directors asked specifically if the activities I used during my training of their staff were written down in any one book. Those comments alone started me thinking about what a valuable staff-training book might be like.

On my transatlantic flight to England, I pulled out an old journal where many of my thoughts are recorded, and began creating a table of contents, a list of valuable activities, and—what is most fun for me—a list of potential titles. *Essential Staff Training Activities* emerged as the winning title. My next step was to enlist the valuable help of some outstanding co-authors.

The second inspiration for this book project is the admiration I have for the efforts made by my co-authors Clare-Marie Hannon and Dave Knobbe of the C5 Youth Foundation. Over the past decade, I've had the opportunity to work with Clare-Marie and Dave dozens of times, and the quality of their programs is inspiring. When it comes to both summer camp programs in general and youth development programs specifically, Clare-Marie and Dave rock. Their input into this project has been considerable.

Dave's inclusion of his team behavior cards was a kind and generous gift to our readers, facilitators, and the adventure-based learning world. Clare-Marie's modification of familiar teambuilding activities specifically for staff-training programs shows the wealth of her knowledge and ability as both a curriculum and training specialist. Even Michael Brandwein was impressed with Clare-Marie's use of activities to reinforce

the concepts in his staff-training books. I am very grateful for their interest and excitement in this project, and their acceptance of my offer to co-author this book with me. I'd also like to express a special thanks to Michael Brandwein for agreeing to write the Foreword of this book.

Finally, my good friend and colleague Mark Norman of the Outward Bound program in Bermuda was kind enough to invite me to his island. Together, we worked with several of Mark's clients on Paget Island, the Outward Bound base camp, near the eastern tip of the Bermuda mainland. In between these programs, I had several days to relax, soak up the sun, swim in amazingly beautiful coastal waters, and write to my heart's content.

Mark is a great host, and in addition to being familiar with the beautiful scenery in Bermuda, he also knows most of the more interesting eateries on the island and where to buy Bermuda Stone Ginger Beer (the island's version of a cross between root beer and ginger ale, with a surprisingly sharp taste). Many bottles were consumed during the writing and editing of this book. I highly recommend it, but you'll have to travel to Bermuda to find it.

As I write these words on Paget Island, here is the view I have. I would suggest exactly such a site for anyone who needs a little inspiration while writing. Rumor has it that J. K. Rowling came to Bermuda to do some of her now-legendary writing. Unfortunately, these photographs do not include the multitude of small green lizards that come by to visit me throughout the day, or the sound of the waves crashing against the rocks on the far side of this inlet, or the occasional sound of boat horns from the nearby harbor, or the warmth of the water (about 86 degrees Fahrenheit today), or the taste of salt in the air from the open ocean, or the playful sound of Mark's dog, Simba, as he swims in the waves (no doubt looking for fish, but never catching any, at least as long as I've been watching). There—have I created a sensory-rich explanation of my surroundings?

In the end, you hold in your hands the final results of a project that was sheer joy for us to create. I hope you'll find these activities valuable in your efforts to make your staff training a bit more active and engaging. And if you happen to have some suggestions of how you make your own staff-training programs lively, please share them with us, and we'll share them with the world.

Jim Cain
Paget Island, Bermuda

Index